Sushi!

Sushi!

**55 Authentic and Innovative Recipes for Nigiri,
Nori-Maki, Chirashi and More!**

Yasuko Fukuoka

AN IMPRINT OF RUNNING PRESS
PHILADELPHIA • LONDON

2003 Salamander Books Ltd

Published by Salamander Books Ltd.

The Chrysalis Building, Bramley Road

London W10 6SP, United Kingdom

This edition published in the United States in 2003 by Courage Books, an imprint of

Running Press Book Publishers

125 South Twenty-second Street

Philadelphia, PA 19103-4399

Visit us on the web!

www.runningpress.com

9 8 7 6 5 4 3 2 1

Library of Congress Control Number: 2002117129

ISBN 0-7624-1636-X

CREDITS

Commissioning Editor: Stella Caldwell

Editor: Anne McDowall

Designer: Cara Hamilton

Photographer: Paul David Ellis

Photographer's Assistant: Martin Holder

Food preparation by: Yasuko Fukuoka, assisted by Kazue Mihara and Ei Kodama

Color reproduction: Anorax Imaging Ltd

Printed in China

ACKNOWLEDGMENTS

Japanese knifes courtesy of Nippon Kitchen, www.nipponkitchen.com

Kodai Nigiri and some other sushi prepared by The Masterchef at JTF.

The author wishes to thank: Nayo and Hiroji Fukuoka, Atsuko Console and Megumi Komiya-Renaud.

Contents

Introduction

For many Western people, "sushi" simply means "raw fish", but the Japanese never eat raw fish by itself: it is always accompanied by condiments or sauces or is marinated, and is invariably served with rice. The best-known form of sushi, nigiri, is a small block of rice topped with raw or marinated fish, shrimp, or other seafood and dipped in shoyu (soy sauce) before eating. Also well known outside Japan is maki-mono or nori-maki: a core of fish, seafood, or vegetables surrounded by a cylinder of rice and coated with nori – seaweed "paper".

Perhaps surprisingly, these styles of sushi are relatively modern: they were devised in Edo (the old name for Tokyo) in the 1820s as an elegant finger food. Sushi actually originated several thousand years ago in China, where cooked fermented rice was used to preserve fish. The fermentation process could last up to five years, after which time the rice was discarded and only the fish eaten. The Japanese adapted this method, reducing the fermentation time and so creating sushi rice or sumeshi: boiled rice seasoned with vinegar, sugar, and salt to emulate the sweet-sour taste of the old style of sushi.

There are now several other distinct types of sushi: oshi-zushi is compressed in a wooden mold and found mainly in the West of Japan; chirashi consists of a bowl of sumeshi rice with various toppings, which are mixed together before eating, and temaki is "DIY" sushi made from rice and several fillings hand rolled in a nori sheet. Numerous "fusion" styles appearing in Japanese sushi bars combine traditional sushi elements and methods with ingredients from Europe, Thailand, and elsewhere.

Sushi is eaten in many different ways in Japan. Nigiri, maki-mono, and sashimi (which is not strictly sushi but slices of raw fish served with shoyu and wasabi, a green spicy paste made from horseradish) are the classic fare of sushi bars and restaurants and are usually accompanied by beer, sake, or green tea. The Japanese love variety in food and rarely eat just one kind of these sushi at a meal.

For example, 6 to 10 pieces of nigiri and half to one thinly rolled maki-mono may be served as a main meal for one.

Oshi-zushi, temaki, and chirashi are home-made styles and are usually served by themselves as main meals. Oshi-zushi is also often taken outdoors as "bento", the classic Japanese lunch box. For temaki the table is laden with plates of ingredients, each diner helping themselves and rolling their own temaki. Chirashi is brought to the table in one large bowl then mixed together, again with each guest helping themselves.

Clear soup (see page 14) may be served with the sushi or at the end of the meal, though never as a course in its own right. Although a dessert is not traditional in Japan, fresh fruit or a fruit sorbet are often enjoyed nowadays.

The Japanese insistence on elegant presentation is particularly apparent in formal meals: hina sushi (see page 91) is a fine example. However, even the less formal and home-made styles are always well presented, as the photographs throughout this book will make clear.

EATING SUSHI

If your chopstick ("hashi") technique is good, all sushi apart from temaki should be eaten with them. If not, nigiri, maki-mono, and oshi-zushi can all be eaten with the fingers, chirashi with a spoon.

To eat nigiri and maki-mono, pick up a piece of nigiri and lightly dip the tip where the topping and the sushi rice meet into a small dish of shoyu. Alternatively, pick up a piece of gari (pickled ginger) using hashi, dip into shoyu, then brush the surface of the sushi with it. For maki-mono, dip (but do not dunk) a corner of a piece into shoyu. Eat gari between pieces to clean your palette. Other sushi is sometimes eaten with shoyu and sometimes without. See individual recipes for instruction.

Ingredients

Japanese cooking makes good use of sun-dried ingredients such as seaweed, fish, and mushrooms. Once used purely as a substitute for fresh ingredients during the winter months, their flavor and nutritional value have expanded their role into becoming a foundation stone in the Japanese diet.

Since Japanese food has become thought of as "healthy food" in the West, most dried and some fresh ingredients have become readily available from Japanese or Oriental food stores, many health food stores, and other specialist food outlets. There are also now many "internet stores" that can deliver Japanese ingredients to your door. Use your web search to find out about e-stores in your country. Suggestions for fresh local ingredients are noted wherever possible.

ABURA-AGE

This is thin tofu fried in oil and is essential for "shojin ryori", vegetarian cooking developed from the diet of Buddhist monks. It is also used opened as a bag to be stuffed with sumeshi rice (see inari, page 89).

AMA-EBI (SWEET RAW SHRIMP)

A type of red shrimp from the Sea of Japan. Unlike other large shrimp that are cooked before serving, ama-ebi are always served raw.

DAIKON RADISH

This white radish is larger and longer than the Western radish. It is also known as mooli in Indian and Caribbean cooking.

DRIED SHIITAKE MUSHROOMS (1)

A strong, pungent mushroom flavor is obtained from these dried mushrooms, which are used extensively in chirashi and soup stocks. After soaking in warm water 2 hours or overnight, dried mushrooms can be used in the same way as fresh ones. (See page 47 for how to cook dried mushrooms for chirashi and maki-mono).

GREEN TEA LEAVES (2)

In Japan, green tea is often served with sushi throughout the meal. Pour hot water into the pot and add 1 teaspoon of tea leaves per person. Brewing time is shorter than for Indian, Ceylon and China tea.

GINGER

The peppery taste and aroma of fresh and pickled ginger was believed to aid the digestion. It also cleans the palate after eating raw fish. Various types are regularly used in Japanese cooking.

Beni-shoga (red pickled ginger) (3)

Shredded ginger pickled in salty liquid, often dyed bright red with food coloring, is used to garnish some chirashi dishes and inari (see page 89). Available from Japanese stores but can be substituted with fresh ginger if unavailable.

Fresh ginger (4)

Used to flavor sumeshi for chirashi or as a condiment to raw fish slices. It should be peeled before use.

Gari (5)

Thinly sliced ginger pickled in sweet and sour liquid. Many sushi recipes feature it as a garnish. When eating different types of raw fish, such as in nigiri, nibble a little gari between pieces to clean your palate. See page 15 for how to prepare this.

Hajikami ginger

A type of ginger that sprouts in shaded spring pools in Japan. The stem and young roots are dug up together. Pickled, dyed, and bottled, it can be found in Japanese stores outside Japan. Gari or beni-shoga can be used instead.

JAPANESE RICE (6)

Short grain and very glutinous when cooked. This stickiness makes rolling, molding, and compressing possible to create sushi. Short-grain white rice makes an acceptable substitute. For directions on how to cook rice and make sumeshi (vinegared rice)—the essential ingredient of almost all sushi—see page 13.

KABAYAKI EEL

Freshwater eel that has been split, cleaned, and broiled with a shoyu-based sauce. Pre-cooked and vacuum-packed kabayaki eel is often available from Japanese stores.

SELECTING FISH FOR SUSHI

Only the freshest fish is suitable for eating raw so it is essential, if you want to make sushi that contain raw fish, that you have a reputable fish market nearby. Although it's not very difficult to prepare fish for sushi at home, almost all Japanese leave the filleting, skinning, and slicing to a skilled fish vendor. Ideally, try to find a good fish market where the vendor knows about sushi, avoid one that sells yesterday's leftovers, or that smells fishy when you stand nearby. It is also worth asking for recommendations for that day's catch.

Quite a wide variety of fish and shellfish can be used as toppings for sushi, provided that it is very fresh. To judge the quality by yourself, check fish for the following:

Eyes should be clear and shiny with no trace of cloudiness
Gills should be bright or bloody red
Scales should be shiny and undamaged
Flesh should be firm and look as if it's still alive
Smell—very fresh fish has none!

KANPYO (7)

A type of gourd, cut into long strips then dried. It can be found in Japanese stores and is often used in maki-mono and chirashi. See page 47 for cooking directions.

KATSUO OR KEZURI BUSHI (8)

Dried bonito tuna shavings used for making dashi stock (see page 13). Often sold in ⅛ ounce packs.

MIRIN (9)

Made from rice and yeast, this sweet seasoning is alcoholic. It is often used in simmered dishes and can be used as an alternative to sugar in cooking.

MISO PASTE

This paste is made from cooked soy beans, grains, and yeast. The best-known dish is miso soup. It is also used to marinate or as a dressing.

RENKON (LOTUS ROOT)

A decorative and edible root that has tubular holes running through it, renkon is used in simmered dishes, tempura, and to decorate chirashi. It is always peeled, parboiled, and soaked in vinegary water a short time before use to remove the bitter juice but is often sold pre-treated and vacuum packed.

RICE VINEGAR (10)

Made from rice and milder than wine or malt vinegar, this is an essential seasoning for sumeshi.

SAKÉ (11)

This rice-based alcoholic drink—pronounced *sah-keh*—is often described as Japanese wine. It has an alcohol content of around 16 percent and is transparent or slightly amber in color. Like wine, the taste can vary from sweet to dry depending on the type of saké. Saké can be served warm or cold but should never be served hot. Kept in an unopened bottle, saké can last up to a year, but once the bottle is opened, the remainder should be kept covered in the refrigerator and consumed within a few days. As well as a drink to accompany sushi and other Japanese food, saké can be used as a seasoning for simmered, steamed, or stewed dishes in the same way that wine is in Western cooking.

SALT (12)

Sea salt is mostly used in Japanese cooking and is essential for seasoning sumeshi.

SALTED EDIBLE CHERRY BLOSSOM AND LEAVES

Freshly picked cherry blossoms and leaves, preserved in salt and used to decorate and infuse dishes. The blossoms can be used in a savoury tea, the leaves to wrap sweet rice dumplings.

SESAME SEEDS (13 AND 14)

Both white and black sesame seeds are widely used, often roasted, which gives them a very nutty flavor. They are often sold ready roasted, but to roast your own, put them in a dry pan over medium heat and stir with a spatula constantly until the seeds begin to pop and release their aroma. This should take 5 to 10 minutes according to quantity.

SHISO LEAVES (15)

A member of the basil and mint family and widely used as a herb in many Japanese dishes, shiso has a refreshing fragrance and peppery aftertaste. It is also sometimes used as garnish as its scalloped leaves are very decorative.

SHOYU (16)

This is the Japanese variety of soy sauce and has a quite different flavor to the Chinese type. It is used extensively in Japanese cooking as a seasoning and also as a dipping sauce, sometimes mixed with wasabi paste, particularly for nigiri and maki-mono (see page 7).

SOBA NOODLES

These buckwheat noodles are served hot or cold with soup or dipping sauces.

SUGAR (17)

Japanese sugar is similar to white granulated sugar and is used in varying quantities for all sumeshi.

TAKUAN

Daikon radish pickled in sweet and salty marinade. Takuan is often dyed yellow with food coloring and is easily obtainable from Japanese or Chinese stores.

WASABI (18)

Japanese horseradish is very hot, giving an explosive spicy heat 10 seconds or so after eating. It is used in nigiri or added to shoyu for dipping slices of raw fish. Wasabi is easy to obtain outside Japan in both powder form and as a ready-mixed paste in a tube. If using powder, mix with the recommended amount of water a few minutes before serving.

YAMA GOBO

This is pickled wild burdock root. Japanese burdock is far less poisonous than the Western type and is always pre-cooked in alkaline liquid to neutralize the bitter juice before using. It is available, only in pickled form, from Japanese stores.

SEAWEED

Seaweed has been an indispensable ingredient in the Japanese diet for centuries. There are many different types used in many different ways, from making soup stock to serving fresh like salad, but all share the distinctive smell of the sea breeze. Seaweed is extremely low in calories and rich in minerals, amino acids, and the much-discussed fucoidan, an anti-cancer and anti-aging substance. Apart from nori, which only lasts a month after opening, dried seaweed can be kept for up to a year in an airtight container and is widely available from Japanese, other Oriental, and health food stores.

Ao-nori (19)

Dried green seaweed flakes used for sushi, other rice dishes, fried noodles, and savory pancakes.

Konbu seaweed (20)

Harvested from the very cold seas surrounding the North of Japan, konbu belongs to the kelp family and can grow up to 100 feet in length. Dried konbu is cut into 12 x 4 inch rectangles and sold packed in this form. It is mainly used to make dashi stock (see page 13), in simmered dishes, and to marinate (or to salt) raw fish. It releases a sticky juice when wet.

Nori dried seaweed (21)

Often used for rolling sushi, the regular 8 x 7 inch nori seaweed sheets are usually sold pre-toasted. Nori should be kept dry in an airtight container or in a sealable plastic bag as it can get damp and quickly lose its flavor. Keep it in the refrigerator and use within a month. Although some flavor is lost, toasting nori can revive dampened nori. To do this, hold 2 sheets of nori in one hand and wave over high heat 5 seconds, making sure that the nori doesn't touch the heat source. Repeat this process a few times until the nori feels and looks dry again.

Tororo or oboro konbu (22)

Made from dried and compressed konbu seaweed, this fluffy shaved konbu can be used in soups and for rolling maki-mono without being soaked in water.

Equipment

Almost all the specialized Japanese cooking tools featured here can be substituted for familiar tools used in the Western kitchen, except for the makisu bamboo rolling mat, which is relatively easy to find.

1 HANDAI

A wooden tub in which to mix cooked rice and seasonings. The wood absorbs excess moisture to create perfect sumeshi. It is also used to mix rice and chirashi ingredients. Soak the tub in water at least 30 minutes before use. A large shallow plastic or ceramic bowl can be used as a substitute.

2 SHAMOJI RICE PADDLE

The bamboo type is for daily use. Always wet before use. Alternatively, use a spatula.

3 FAN

Used to cool sumeshi quickly, making rice shiny and tasty.

4 MAKISU

A rolling mat made of bamboo sticks woven together with cotton threads. An essential tool for making maki-mono, it can be found in Oriental stores.

5 OMELET PAN

A square or rectangular pan is used to make usuyaki and atsuyaki omelets (see pages 14 and 27). A round skillet can also be used to make Japanese omelets.

6 LACQUERED CHOPSTICKS

For use at the table, the non-slip types have a rough surface at the tip making them easy to use. Find them at Oriental stores.

7 WOODEN OR BAMBOO CHOPSTICKS

Long ones are for cooking, short ones for eating with. Find them at Oriental stores, good kitchenware retailers or make your own from bamboo.

8 SASHIMI KNIFE

A long thin blade makes this knife effective for slicing fish. A carving knife can also be used. For best results, always sharpen with a whetstone before use.

9 CHEF'S KNIFE

The multi-purpose Japanese knife, also useful for Western cooking. Again, a carving knife is an acceptable substitute.

10 OSHI-GATA

A wooden mold for making oshi-zushi (see page 65). Wet well before use. Plastic and glass containers with lids can be used instead: line with a piece of plastic wrap 50 percent larger than the inside of the mold or container to cover the top and make the oshi-zushi easier to lift out.

11 SUSHI-DAI

A traditional wooden plate on which to serve nigiri or maki-mono, often used in sushi restaurants and bars.

12 MOSSO-GATA

Used to mold cooked rice for bento, the Japanese lunch box. Usually larger than a cookie cutter, which can be used as a substitute.

13 JAPANESE DISHCLOTH

Made with thin cotton and often printed with a traditional design, this is used wet to cover sumeshi to prevent it from drying out. A cotton or linen dish cloth will suffice.

14 JAPANESE GRATER

Made from ceramic, metal, or plastic, this is finer than the Western cheese grater. When shredded with this, daikon radish has the texture of having been blended in a food processor. The latter can be used as a substitute.

Basic Recipes and Techniques

Sumeshi—from "su", vinegar, and "meshi", cooked rice, and sometimes called sushi-meshi—is the fundamental ingredient in all sushi recipes. Cooked sumeshi should normally be used the same day. Never keep leftover sumeshi in the refrigerator as the rice dries out and becomes unsuitable for use. It doesn't freeze well either. The best way to recycle leftover sumeshi is to keep it at room temperature and use it to make mushi zushi (see page 60) the following day.

There are also several other basic recipes and techniques that are used in making sushi. Most of these are given here; some others (such as atsuyaki omelet, see page 27) are featured and cross-referred to elsewhere in the book.

SUMESHI RICE (VINEGARED RICE FOR SUSHI)

MAKES 2 ½ POUNDS

2 ½ CUPS JAPANESE RICE OR PUDDING RICE
4 ½ TABLESPOONS RICE VINEGAR
2 TABLESPOONS SUGAR
1 TEASPOON SALT

◆ Wash rice with cold water, changing water 3 or 4 times until it runs clear. Drain into a strainer and leave an hour.
◆ Mix vinegar, sugar, and salt in a jar. Stir until dissolved.
◆ Transfer rice into a medium-size pan (around 6 ½ inch diameter) with 5 parts cold water to 4 parts rice.
◆ Cover pan and bring to boil. Immediately reduce heat to low and simmer 10 minutes or until you hear a faint crackling noise. Remove pan from heat and let stand an additional 10 minutes without lifting the lid.
◆ Transfer rice to a large bowl and drizzle vinegar mixture all over it. Hold a spatula as you would hold a knife and "slice" rice many times until thoroughly vinegared, but do not stir it. Use a fan to cool rice quickly to room temperature.
Note: The composition of the vinegar mix varies in certain recipes. Follow quantities given in each recipe.

DASHI STOCK

Dashi stock is a Japanese soup stock made from dried ingredients. This stock is widely used in Japanese cooking. You can also use instant dashi granules. Follow the directions on the package to make the required amount of stock.

4 INCH PIECE DRIED KONBU SEAWEED
2 CUPS (OR 6 X ⅛ OUNCE PACKS) KATSUO OR KEZURI BUSHI

◆ Put konbu seaweed into a pan with 2 ½ cups water and let soak at least an hour or overnight.
◆ Put the pan on a moderate heat and remove just before it reaches boiling point.
◆ Add katsuo or kezuri bushi, heat again, and remove just before boiling. Wait until it has settled, then strain into a bowl. This liquid in the bowl is called the "first stock" and is used for clear soup.
◆ The remainder in the strainer can be put back into the pan with another 2 ½ cups water and simmered without a lid over a moderate heat 15 minutes. Strain as for the first stock. This is the "second stock" and is used mainly for noodle soup and other dishes.

CLEAR SOUP WITH
WAKAME SEAWEED

Japanese soups are divided into two categories. One is miso soup, using soy bean paste, and is served at breakfast and with other home meals. The other is the clear soup that is often included in a traditional tea ceremony dinner and with sushi dishes.

Seaweed, shellfish, fish or chicken, mushrooms, and tofu can all be added to this clear soup if desired.

MAKES 4 SERVINGS

A SMALL HANDFUL DRIED WAKAME SEAWEED
1 GREEN ONION, FINELY CHOPPED
5 CUPS DASHI STOCK
1 ½ TABLESPOONS SHOYU
SALT

◆ Soak wakame in 1 cup water 15 minutes and drain the water.
◆ Heat dashi stock in a pan. When it boils, add wakame and simmer 2 minutes.
◆ Season with shoyu and salt to taste, then remove from heat. Sprinkle with chopped green onion and serve immediately.

USUYAKI (THIN) OMELET
MAKES 6 TO 8 THIN OMELETS

4 EGGS, LIGHTLY BEATEN
½ TEASPOON SALT
VEGETABLE OIL

◆ Season beaten eggs with salt. Heat ½ tablespoon oil in a Japanese square omelet pan or ordinary skillet until very hot. Remove pan from heat and wipe up excess oil with absorbent kitchen paper.
◆ Put pan back over a medium heat. Pour just enough egg into the pan to completely cover the surface. When the surface of the omelet looks dry, remove from heat again and lift omelet with a skewer. Turn it over and move to a plate when it looks dry again.

SLICING FISH

For nigiri and other sushi, ask your fish vendor to fillet the fish for you. Most large fish such as tuna or salmon are sold in the West as steaks, cut across the grain. This is not the ideal shape for sushi or sashimi (raw fish slices served with garnish). Trim skinned fillet into an even rectangular slab. If using a steak, ask your fish vendor to cut it at least ½ inch thick, then trim it down to short rectangular slabs.

◆ Place the fillet skin side up on a chopping board. Cut straight along the grain into slices ⅛ to ½ inch thick. Flat fish, such as turbot or flounder, or firm white fish, such as sea bream, black bream, red snapper, or sea bass, are better thinly sliced, whereas fish such as tuna, yellow-tail, swordfish, or salmon are better thickly sliced.

◆ If the fillet itself is thinner than 1 inch, a vertical cut would make too narrow a slice to use for nigiri. In this case, instead of holding the knife vertically, cut through the fillet at a 45-degree angle to make a wider slice.

◆ For maki-mono and temaki, cut all fish into ½ inch square long rectangular strips. One maki-mono roll will require strips 8 inches long; cut 2 or 3 shorter strips to make up the length as necessary. Temaki requires rectangles of about ½ inch square and 3 inches long.

GARI

8 OUNCES FRESH GINGER, PEELED
5 TABLESPOONS RICE VINEGAR
2 ½ TABLESPOONS SUGAR
1 TEASPOON SALT
½ TEASPOON RED FOOD COLORING (OPTIONAL)

◆ Slice ginger very thinly with a sharp knife or vegetable slicer. Soak in cold water 10 minutes, then drain.
◆ Mix and dissolve all seasonings in a plastic or glass jar with a lid. Add food coloring if pink-colored gari is preferred.
◆ Cook ginger slices in boiling water over a medium heat until translucent. Drain and put into the seasoning mix immediately.
◆ Leave ginger to pickle at least 3 hours.
◆ Home-made gari can be kept in the jar in the refrigerator about 2 weeks.

RADISH FLOWERS

Presentation is a very important part of Japanese cuisine. These radish flowers are used in hina sushi (see page 91) and could also be used to garnish other dishes.

8 RADISHES, PEELED, STEMS REMOVED
1 TABLESPOON RICE VINEGAR
1 TEASPOON SUGAR
PINCH SALT
RED FOOD COLORING (OPTIONAL)

◆ Shave bottoms of radishes so that they stand upright. On a chopping board, stand a radish between 2 horizontally placed chopsticks. Make 6 to 8 downward cuts along length of radish until blade touches chopsticks. Turn radish 90 degrees and make another 6 to 8 cuts across ones already made.
◆ In a small bowl, mix together rice vinegar, sugar, and a pinch of salt. Pour half of this marinade mixture into another small bowl and add a few drops of red food coloring to one bowl. Place 4 radishes in each bowl and let marinate 30 minutes.
◆ Drain radishes and open the cuts with your fingers.

Nigiri

[Molded Sushi]

Nigiri sushi consists of a hand-molded rectangular block of sushi rice, topped with various raw fish slices, shellfish, or omelet. This is one of the most familiar styles of sushi in the West. At a sushi bar, you can sit at a wooden counter table and eat as soon as the chef makes nigiri with toppings of your choice. This is the best way to eat nigiri sushi, which began its life as a "street food for the rich" in Tokyo about 180 years ago.

The Japanese tend not to make nigiri sushi at home. However, it is not too difficult to turn your home into a sushi bar if you can find very fresh fish (see page 10), Japanese rice, and a sharp knife. Molding nigiri should be done just before serving and eating; once sliced, raw fish doesn't keep fresh until the next day.

HOW TO ROLL NIGIRI

1 Take 2 tablespoons of sumeshi rice and squeeze it in the palm of your hand to make a firm rice ball. Pick up a slice of fish in your other hand and lay it across the palm of your hand.

2 Smear the center of the slice of fish with a little wasabi paste to taste.

Place rice ball on fish and quickly press rice into fish with your forefinger and middle finger.

3 Turn sushi over and finish shaping it into a 2 inch long rectangular block. Repeat until all fish slices are molded into nigiri.

Several recipes in this book refer to "nigiri-shaped rice blocks". These are made by following the steps above but leaving out the fish.

Maguro Nigiri [Raw Tuna Nigiri]

MAKES 24 PIECES

5 OUNCES EACH LEAN (AKAMI), FATTY (CHU-TORO) AND EXTRA FATTY (OH-TORO) TUNA FILLET, SKINNED (SEE NOTE)

RICE VINEGAR

SUMESHI RICE (SEE PAGE 13) MADE WITH ¾ CUP RICE MIXED WITH 2 TABLESPOONS RICE VINEGAR, 2 TEASPOONS SUGAR, AND A PINCH OF SALT

2 TABLESPOONS WASABI PASTE

¼ CUP GARI, TO GARNISH

4 SHISO LEAVES, TO GARNISH

SHOYU, TO SERVE

◆ Trim tuna fillets to a rectangular shape (see page 15). Using a sharp carving knife, cut crosswise into ¼ inch thick slices.

◆ Fill a bowl with equal quantities of water and rice vinegar to wet or wash hands. Place tuna slices, sumeshi rice, and wasabi at hand.

◆ Following directions on page 17, mold rice and a slice of tuna into nigiri. Make 8 pieces from each of the 3 different types of tuna.

◆ Lay a shiso leaf on each of 4 individual dishes. Arrange nigiri on leaves and garnish with gari. Serve with a little dish of shoyu.

Note: If these varieties of tuna are not available, use 1 pound fresh tuna fillet.

Two-Color Nigiri

MAKES 32 PIECES

*7 OUNCES SALMON FILLET,
SKINNED AND BONED*

*7 OUNCES SQUID, BODY ONLY,
CLEANED, SKINNED, AND BONED*

*SUMESHI RICE (SEE PAGE 13) MADE WITH
1 1/2 CUPS RICE MIXED WITH 2 1/2 TABLESPOONS
RICE VINEGAR, 1 TABLESPOON SUGAR,
AND 1/2 TEASPOON SALT*

*1 TO 2 TABLESPOONS FRESHLY MIXED
WASABI PASTE*

*8 SHISO LEAVES,
CUT IN HALF LENGTHWISE*

GARI, TO GARNISH

DIPPING SAUCE

1/4 CUP SHOYU

1 TABLESPOON FINELY SNIPPED CHIVES

1/2 LEMON, CUT INTO 4

◆ Sprinkle salmon with salt and let stand 30 minutes. Wipe with absorbent kitchen paper and slice crosswise into 1/3 inch thick pieces. Slice squid crosswise into 1 inch wide ribbons.

◆ Mix a cupful each of water and rice vinegar in a bowl to use for wetting your hands. Scoop 1 1/2 tablespoons of sumeshi rice into your hand and mold into a 2 inch oval shape. Smear a little wasabi on top.

◆ Follow basic directions for nigiri (see page 17) to make salmon pieces. For squid nigiri, stick a shiso leaf onto sumeshi rice before pressing on topping. Make 16 pieces of each type of nigiri.

◆ To make dipping sauce, pour 1 tablespoon shoyu into each of 4 individual small dishes. Squeeze in lemon juice and add chives.

◆ Arrange sushi on serving dishes. Serve garnished with gari and accompanied by individual dishes of dipping sauce.

Sakura Nigiri [Cherry Blossom Nigiri]

*2 SHEETS KONBU SEAWEED,
EACH 6 INCHES LONG*

*7 OUNCES VERY FRESH WHITE FISH ,
SUCH AS FLOUNDER, TURBOT, OR BREAM,
SKINNED AND FILLETED*

*SUMESHI RICE (SEE PAGE 13) MADE WITH
¾ CUP RICE MIXED WITH 4 TEASPOONS RICE
VINEGAR, 2 TEASPOONS SUGAR, A PINCH OF
SALT, AND A FEW DROPS RED FOOD COLORING*

1 TO 2 TABLESPOONS WASABI PASTE

*8 SALTED EDIBLE CHERRY BLOSSOM FLOWERS,
SOAKED IN WATER UNTIL NEEDED*

*8 SALTED EDIBLE CHERRY LEAVES (SEE NOTE)
AND GARI, TO GARNISH*

SHOYU, TO SERVE

◆ Wipe konbu sheets with a damp cloth then put fish fillet on one sheet. Cover with second sheet and wrap very tightly in plastic wrap. Let stand at least an hour.

◆ Remove konbu sheets from fish and slice thinly as for sushi topping (see page 15). Keep the 8 best-looking ones; the rest can be eaten as sashimi (see page 7).

◆ Make 16 pieces of nigiri rice following the basic directions on page 17. Put a little smear of wasabi on top, place one fish slice on the palm of your hand, and remold with rice. Repeat this to make 8 pieces. Wrap the other 8 nigiri rice pieces with edible cherry leaves.

◆ Scoop a cherry blossom flower from the water with a dessertspoon and carefully move it onto a piece of absorbent kitchen paper.

◆ Arrange pieces of white fish nigiri and cherry leaf wrapped nigiri on individual serving plates. Garnish each fish nigiri with a salted cherry blossom flower and a piece of gari and serve with individual small dishes of shoyu.

Note: If cherry leaves are unavailable, use Greek salted vine leaves or spring greens boiled in salted water and cut into 3 inch wide strips.

Shojin Nigiri [Vegetarian Nigiri]

MAKES 20 PIECES

1 LARGE RED BELL PEPPER

2 TABLESPOONS SAKÉ

1 TEASPOON SALT

½ CARROT, PEELED AND THINLY SLICED
LENGTHWISE INTO AT LEAST 8 STRIPS

1 INCH RENKON (LOTUS ROOT), SLICED INTO
⅛ INCH THICK DISKS

8 ASPARAGUS SPEARS, CUT INTO 3 INCH PIECES

4 OKRA, THICK END TRIMMED

4 LARGE FLAT MUSHROOMS

1 TABLESPOON SHOYU

½ TABLESPOON MIRIN

SUMESHI RICE (SEE PAGE 13) MADE WITH
1 CUP RICE MIXED WITH 2 TABLESPOONS
RICE VINEGAR, 1 TABLESPOON SUGAR, AND
½ TEASPOON SALT

½ NORI SHEET, CUT IN HALF, THEN INTO
½ INCH WIDE STRIPS LENGTHWISE

DIPPING SAUCE

¼ CUP SHOYU

1 TABLESPOON BALSAMIC VINEGAR

2 TABLESPOONS SNIPPED CHIVES

◆ Heat oven to 400F and cook bell pepper about 30 minutes until skin starts to burn. Peel and de-seed, then trim into four 3 x 1½ inch rectangles.

◆ Half fill a large pan with cold water and add saké, salt, and carrot. Bring to a boil and simmer over moderate heat 7 minutes. Using a slotted spoon, remove carrot and set aside.

◆ Add renkon, asparagus, and okra and simmer 5 minutes. Drain, reserving 1¼ cups cooking liquid for cooking mushrooms plus 2 tablespoons for dipping sauce.

◆ Simmer mushrooms in reserved cooking liquid with shoyu and mirin 15 minutes. Drain, remove stalks, and trim mushrooms to make 3 x 1½ inch rectangles, scoring surface in a grid pattern.

◆ Make 20 nigiri rice blocks (see page 17). Wipe off excess moisture from vegetables with absorbent kitchen paper.

◆ Cover 4 rice blocks with a piece of red bell pepper, 4 with mushroom, 4 with carrot, 4 with okra, and 4 with asparagus. Wrap a nori strip round pepper and asparagus nigiri. Lay renkon slices on carrot nigiri and wrap each okra nigiri with a strip of carrot.

◆ To make dipping sauce, mix together shoyu, balsamic vinegar, snipped chives, and remaining 2 tablespoons of vegetable cooking liquid.

Ebi Ikomi [Jumbo Shrimp Stuffed with Rice]

MAKES 8 PIECES

8 RAW JUMBO SHRIMP, UNPEELED,
HEADS AND TAILS LEFT ON

2 EGGS, LIGHTLY BEATEN

3 TABLESPOONS RICE VINEGAR

1 TEASPOON SUGAR

PINCH SALT

SUMESHI RICE (SEE PAGE 13) MADE WITH
2/3 CUP RICE MIXED WITH 1 TABLESPOON
RICE VINEGAR, 1 TEASPOON SUGAR, AND
A PINCH OF SALT

8 SHISO LEAVES

◆ Insert a bamboo skewer lengthwise into each shrimp to prevent curling and boil in salted water 3 minutes. Leave in pan until cooled.

◆ Remove skewers and shell shrimp, leaving heads and tails on. Insert a carving knife across spine to slit open body. Try not to damage heads and tails.

◆ Pour beaten egg through a strainer into a pan and add rice vinegar, sugar, and salt. Using 4 to 5 chopsticks or a fork, stir over moderate to low heat to make powdery scrambled egg. (This can take about 15 minutes.)

◆ Fill a container 1/2 inch deep with egg and add shrimp. Cover with more egg and marinate at least 3 hours.

◆ Take out shrimp and dust off egg, reserving egg. Stuff 1 tablespoon sumeshi rice into slit of each shrimp.

◆ Place shiso leaves on a serving dish, lay shrimp on top, and sprinkle with egg to serve.

Hotate Nigiri [Scallop Nigiri]

MAKES 8 PIECES

SUMESHI RICE (SEE PAGE 13) MADE WITH
2/3 CUP RICE MIXED WITH 1 TABLESPOON RICE
VINEGAR, 1 TEASPOON SUGAR, AND A PINCH OF
SALT (SEE NOTE)

8 FRESH SCALLOPS, SHELLED,
FRILL AND CORAL REMOVED

1 CUCUMBER, HALVED LENGTHWISE
AND CUT VERY THINLY INTO HALF-MOON DISKS

1 TO 2 TABLESPOONS WASABI PASTE

GARI, SHOYU, AND ZEST 1 LIME, TO SERVE

◆ Slice each scallop nearly in half horizontally. Stop slicing at ligament that joins shell to muscle meat. Open cut and rest on a plate, cut side down. The ligament should look like a hinge connecting the 2 slices of meat.

◆ Following nigiri directions on page 17, mold rice and press on scallops.

◆ Put scallop nigiri on a plate and decorate with cucumber disks arranged like a fan. Serve with gari and dip into a little plate of shoyu sprinkled with lime zest.

Note: This quantity of sumeshi rice is more than is actually needed for this recipe, but it is difficult to cook a small quantity of rice.

Kodai Nigiri [Old Edo-Style Nigiri]

1 SQUID, BODY ONLY, SKINNED AND BONED

8 MEDIUM SCALLOPS, CORAL REMOVED

3 ½ OUNCES LEAN TUNA

SHOYU

1 MARINATED MACKEREL FILLET (SEE PAGE 66)

SUMESHI RICE (SEE PAGE 13) MADE WITH
1 ⅓ CUPS RICE MIXED WITH 2 ½ TABLESPOONS
RICE VINEGAR, 1 TABLESPOON SUGAR,
AND ½ TEASPOON SALT

1 TO 2 TABLESPOONS FRESHLY MIXED
WASABI PASTE

5 OUNCE BLACK BREAM FILLET,
SPRINKLED WITH SALT

¼ NORI SHEET CUT INTO STRIPS
½ INCH WIDE

GARI, TO GARNISH

TSUME SAUCE

½ CUP SHOYU

½ CUP MIRIN

1 TABLESPOON SUGAR

◆ To make tsume sauce, put shoyu, mirin, and sugar in a small saucepan and bring to a boil. Boil vigorously 5 minutes, then add squid and boil 1 to 2 minutes. Cool in the pan.

◆ Remove squid from pan with a slotted spoon and score surface with a sharp knife. Cut in half lengthwise and slice into 1 ½ inch wide strips crosswise.

◆ Put scallops into the same pan and boil 1 minute. Remove from pan with a slotted spoon and dry on absorbent kitchen paper. Cut in half horizontally.

◆ Cut tuna, bream, and mackerel across the grain into ½ inch thick rectangular slices. Separate tuna and put into a small bowl, adding enough shoyu to cover slices, and let marinate 15 minutes.

◆ Bring sauce to a boil again and boil vigorously until almost caramelized. Cool.

◆ Using a slice of fish, piece of squid, or a scallop and 1 tablespoon of rice for each, mold nigiri following directions on page 17.

◆ Wrap a strip of nori around each squid and scallop nigiri. Arrange nigiri on a large tray or on 4 individual plates. Brush a little tsume sauce on squid, black bream, and scallop nigiri. Serve with gari.

Note: This old style nigiri is eaten without dipping in shoyu.

Gyu Nigiri [Beef Slice]

MAKES 24 PIECES

14 OUNCES BEEF FILLET OR SIRLOIN STEAKS

SALT

SUMESHI RICE (SEE PAGE 13) MADE WITH
2/3 CUP RICE MIXED WITH 1 TABLESPOON
RICE VINEGAR, 1 TEASPOON SUGAR, AND
A PINCH OF SALT

2 TABLESPOONS WASABI PASTE

DIPPING SAUCE

1/4 CUP SHOYU

2 TABLESPOONS MIRIN

1 GARLIC CLOVE, VERY FINELY CHOPPED

1 SMALL APPLE, PEELED AND SHREDDED

2 GREEN ONIONS, FINELY CHOPPED

2 TABLESPOONS WHITE SESAME SEEDS, TOASTED

CONDIMENTS

2 INCH PIECE DAIKON RADISH, PEELED AND
FINELY SHREDDED

2 TEASPOONS DIJON-STYLE MUSTARD

2 SHISO LEAVES, FINELY CHOPPED
JUST BEFORE SERVING

1 PACK MUSTARD CRESS, STALKS CUT
1 INCH FROM TOP

◆ Sprinkle beef with salt and let stand 10 minutes.

◆ To make dipping sauce, place shoyu, mirin, garlic, and 2 tablespoons water in a saucepan and bring to boil. Remove pan from heat and stir in shredded apple, green onion, and sesame seeds. Cool.

◆ Mix shredded daikon and mustard together in a small bowl and set aside until required.

◆ Sear beef in a very hot dry skillet 1 minute on each side. Plunge into a bowl of ice cold water to prevent further cooking. Dry with absorbent kitchen paper and cut as if slicing fish for nigiri toppings (see page 15).

◆ Following directions on page 17, mold 1 1/2 tablespoons sumeshi rice and a slice of beef together, dabbing beef with a little wasabi paste.

◆ Arrange nigiri on a large plate and decorate with a pinch each of mustard-flavored daikon, chopped shiso leaves, and mustard cress. Put remaining condiments into separate bowls.

◆ Serve with dipping sauce on individual small plates and ask guests to mix condiments of their choice into the sauce.

Tamago Nigiri [Atsuyaki Omelet Nigiri]

MAKES 24 PIECES

*Sumeshi rice (see page 13) made with
1 ⅓ cups rice mixed with 2 tablespoons
rice vinegar, 1 tablespoon sugar,
and ½ teaspoon salt*

4 shiso leaves, cut in half lengthwise

Gari and shoyu, to serve

ATSUYAKI OMELET

¼ cup dashi stock (see page 13)

2 tablespoons saké

4 teaspoons sugar

½ teaspoon salt

6 eggs, lightly beaten

Vegetable oil

◆ To make atsuyaki omelets, mix dashi stock, saké, sugar, and salt into a bowl and stir in beaten eggs. Divide egg mixture into 2 bowls to make 2 omelets.

◆ Heat a Japanese square pan or a round skillet. When hot, reduce heat and wipe with oiled kitchen paper.

◆ Pour in one third of the mixture from one bowl. Tilt pan to spread evenly. Wait until egg is nearly cooked then fold toward the handle with chopsticks or a spatula. If using a round pan, fold 1 inch from left and right sides into the center, then fold toward the handle.

◆ Keeping rolled egg near the handle, oil the bottom again. Slide rolled egg to the opposite end of the pan, then pour in half the remaining egg mixture. Tilt the pan to spread egg, including beneath first roll. Fold in the same way as before.

◆ Pour on remaining mixture and repeat the process to create a thick 3-layer omelet. Turn omelet out onto a chopping board. Repeat to make a second omelet. Cut each omelet into half lengthwise then into 6 crosswise.

◆ To make nigiri, insert a knife crosswise into the center of each piece of omelet to make a pocket. Slide in one shiso leaf and spoon about 2 to 3 tablespoons of rice into the pocket. Serve with gari and shoyu.

Edomae Nigiri [Edo-style Assorted Nigiri]

Sumeshi rice (see page 13) made with 1 ⅓ cups rice mixed with 2 ½ tablespoons rice vinegar, 1 tablespoon sugar, and ½ teaspoon salt

14 ounces assorted fresh fish fillets and shellfish, such as flounder, tuna, bream, salmon, cooked octopus tentacles, marinated mackerel (see page 66), kabayaki eel (pre-cooked), and scallops (see Hotate Nigiri, page 23)

¼ cup wasabi paste

8 shiso leaves, to garnish

Gari and shoyu, to serve

◆ Ask your fish vendor to cut all fish into fillets, boned and skinned. Trim both sides at home to make each fillet into a rectangular block.

◆ Following the directions on page 15, slice fish into nigiri topping shapes. Cut flat fish (e.g. flounder or turbot) into ¼ inch slices, tuna, salmon and bream into ⅓ inch slices. Cut octopus tentacles diagonally crosswise. Make 4 slices of each kind.

◆ Fill a small bowl with equal quantities of water and rice vinegar for wetting hands. Place all toppings, sumeshi rice and wasabi paste ready at hand.

◆ Mold 1½ tablespoons sumeshi rice and a topping into nigiri following directions on page 17. Smear wasabi on rice blocks to taste.

◆ Arrange nigiri on individual plates or in a handai rice tub (see page 12). Garnish with shiso leaves and serve immediately with gari and a little dish of shoyu.

Note: Large raw shrimp (heads removed), ama-ebi sweet shrimp (peeled and heads removed), squid or cuttlefish, and turbot would also be suitable for this recipe.

Maki-Mono
[Rolled Sushi]

Maki-mono means "rolled things". Sumeshi rice is rolled around various fillings using a makisu, a Japanese bamboo rolling mat. Although the rolling technique looks complicated, it's not difficult to learn, and maki-mono makes great finger food for parties. The filling may include raw or cooked fish, cooked vegetables, such as shiitake mushrooms or kanpyo (dried gourd), or raw vegetables and pickles. The filled rice roll is most usually wrapped in a nori seaweed sheet.

Maki-mono is generally made in one of two sizes: the thin-rolled hoso maki (see page 34), which contains one or two kinds of fillings, or the thicker futo maki (see page 33), which can contain as many as 10 different fillings and can be up to 6 inches in diameter. Hoso maki is also combined with nigiri in assembling an assorted sushi platter. Six to eight pieces of nigiri sushi and a half roll each of two kinds of hoso maki are often served per person as a main course in Japan.

ROLLING MAKI-MONO

1 Place the makisu bamboo rolling mat on a work surface. The line of bamboo sticks should be laid horizontally towards you. Lay a nori sheet, shiny side down, longer edge towards you, onto the makisu bamboo mat. Make sure the nearest edge of the nori is lined up with the edge of the makisu.

Scoop a generous handful of sumeshi rice–or a half handful for hoso maki–and spread it onto the nori sheet, smoothing it out evenly with wet fingers. Leave the far 3/4 inch (1/4 inch for hoso maki) clear. Make a trench along the centre with your finger in which to place core fillings.

2 Lay one or more fillings of your choice in the trench and straighten them.

3 Holding the makisu mat with your thumbs while holding fillings in place with your ring fingers, roll the near edge of the mat forwards until it touches the clear space at the top of the nori. Lift the rolled edge of the mat from the sushi itself and continue to roll until you reach the end.

Some wrappings, such as omelet, don't naturally stick together. Use some crushed sumeshi rice to stick ends and prevent the maki-mono from unrolling.

Just before serving, slice the rolls with a sharp wet knife, wiping it clean after each cut.

Futo Maki [Thick-rolled Sushi]

6 TO 8 DRIED SHIITAKE MUSHROOMS

10G (¼OZ) DRIED KANPYO GOURD

7 NORI SHEETS

SUMESHI RICE (SEE PAGE 13) MADE WITH
1 ½ CUPS RICE MIXED WITH 3 ½ TABLESPOONS
RICE VINEGAR, 1 ½ TABLESPOONS SUGAR,
AND 2 TEASPOONS SALT

1 CUCUMBER, CUT INTO ½ INCH SQUARE
STRAIGHT LONG STICKS

ATSUYAKI OMELET (SEE PAGE 27) MADE WITH
3 EGGS, ½ TABLESPOON SAKÉ, 2 TEASPOONS
SUGAR, AND A PINCH SALT, CUT INTO STRIPS
½ INCH SQUARE X 8 INCHES LONG

⅓ CUP RED LUMPFISH CAVIAR

1 TAKUAN (PICKLED DAIKON RADISH),
CUT INTO ½ INCH SQUARE LONG STICKS

1 PACK PRE-SEASONED ABURA-AGE
(THIN FRIED TOFU: USE 3 OR 4 PIECES, LAYERED
AND CUT INTO ½ INCH WIDE STRIPS)

1 KABAYAKI EEL (PRE-COOKED EEL),
CUT INTO ½ INCH SQUARES

⅔ CUP BENI-SHOGA (RED PICKLED GINGER),
DRAINED

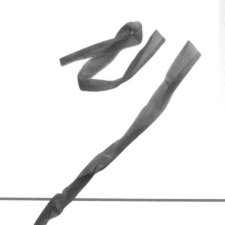

◆ Cook shiitake and kanpyo according to basic chirashi mix directions (see page 47). Drain well, remove stalks from shiitake, and slice caps thinly. Cut kanpyo into strips 8 inches long.

◆ Place 4 sheets of nori to one side. Cut one third off 2 other sheets so they measure 4½ x 8 inches. Cut remainder lengthwise to create 8 x 1 inch ribbons.

◆ Put a makisu mat on the work surface, smooth side down with the long edge toward you. Mix a cupful of water in a bowl with a similar amount of rice vinegar to use for wetting or washing your hands.

◆ Lay a whole nori sheet, shiny side down, long edge toward you, on the mat, lining up front edge of nori with the edge of the makisu.

◆ Scoop a handful of sumeshi and spread it onto the nori sheet, smoothing it out with wet fingers. Leave the top ¾ inch clear. Make a groove horizontally across the center with your finger in which to place fillings.

◆ Take a 4½ x 8 inch sheet of nori and lay it over the rice, pressing it into the groove, leaving the top third of the rice uncovered.

◆ Lay shiitake slices and kanpyo gourd strips next to each other across rice. Neatly layer a stick each of cucumber and takuan, a piece each of abura-age, kabayaki eel, and pickled ginger, and 1 omelet strip on top of shiitake and kanpyo gourds strips.

◆ Roll up following directions on page 31. Leave rolled in the mat a few minutes, then unroll and set aside. Repeat to make another roll.

◆ Individually wrap all remaining fillings in nori ribbons. Put sumeshi rice on a nori sheet as before, making a groove in the center again. Scatter 1 tablespoon lumpfish caviar on rice. Lay individually wrapped fillings on rice as above and roll up. Repeat to make another roll.

◆ Just before serving, slice rolls with a sharp wet knife. First cut roll in half, then cut each half into 4 equal pieces.

◆ Arrange on serving dishes and garnish with red pickled ginger. Futo maki is normally eaten with the fingers without dipping in shoyu.

Hoso Maki [Thin-rolled Sushi]

MAKES 48 PIECES

2 SMALL OR 1 LARGE CUCUMBER

*1 TAKUAN (PICKLED DAIKON RADISH)
ABOUT 8 INCHES LONG*

4 OUNCE SMOKED SALMON SLICE

4 OUNCE SMOKED HALIBUT SLICE

*SUMESHI RICE (SEE PAGE 13) MADE WITH
1 ⅓ CUPS RICE MIXED WITH 2 TABLESPOONS
RICE VINEGAR, 1 TABLESPOON SUGAR,
AND ½ TEASPOON SALT*

2 TABLESPOONS WASABI PASTE

*4 NORI SHEETS, CUT IN HALF TO MAKE
8 X 3 ½ INCH RECTANGLES*

GARI AND SHOYU, TO SERVE

◆ Cut cucumber and takuan into matchsticks 2 to 4 inches long and as straight as possible.

◆ Cut salmon and halibut into ½ inch wide strips lengthwise.

◆ Have prepared vegetables, fish, sumeshi, and wasabi paste ready at hand. Following directions on page 31, lay a nori sheet on a makisu rolling mat and spread ⅓ cup sumeshi rice on top. Smear a little wasabi paste across the center.

◆ Lay a strip of cucumber and takuan on top of each other along the line of wasabi.

◆ Lift the makisu with both thumbs and roll at once. Unwrap the mat and repeat to make another 3 rolls.

◆ Repeat as above, but replace cucumber and takuan with smoked salmon and halibut strips to make another 4 rolls.

◆ Cut each roll into 6 pieces just before serving. Serve with gari and a little dish of shoyu.

Shojin Maki [Pickled Vegetable Roll]

MAKES 72 PIECES

6 NORI SHEETS, CUT IN HALF CROSSWISE

SUMESHI RICE (SEE PAGE 13) MADE WITH
2 CUPS RICE MIXED WITH 3 ½ TABLESPOONS
RICE VINEGAR, 1 ½ TABLESPOONS SUGAR,
AND 1 ½ TEASPOONS SALT

2 SMALL OR 1 LARGE CUCUMBER,
CUT INTO ½ INCH SQUARE STICKS

1 TAKUAN (PICKLED DAIKON RADISH),
ABOUT 8 INCHES LONG, CUT INTO
½ INCH SQUARE LONG STICKS

5 TO 7 PIECES YAMA GOBO (PICKLED BURDOCK),
CUT IN HALF LENGTHWISE

⅔ CUP PICKLED CUCUMBER WITH SESAME
SEEDS, DRAINED AND FINELY CHOPPED

GARI, TO SERVE

◆ Place a makisu bamboo rolling mat on the work surface. Lay a sheet of nori on it and spread about ⅓ cup of sumeshi rice evenly over the surface using wet fingers.

◆ Put a cucumber stick in the center of the rice and roll (see opposite). Make 3 of these rolls.

◆ Repeat the process to make 3 rolls with takuan, 3 with yama gobo, and 3 with pickled cucumber. For the latter, use a spoon to draw a guide line on the rice and place the fillings along it.

◆ Cut each roll into 6 pieces with a sharp knife and serve with gari.

Note: You can buy all the pickles used here from a Japanese store, but if you are unable to obtain them, try other preserved vegetables or pickles, finely chopped black olives, or stalks of broccoli, peeled, cut into ½ inch square sticks, and marinated overnight in miso paste.

Hana Maki [Flower Roll]

MAKES 36 PIECES

1 RED BELL PEPPER

9 LARGE RAW SHRIMP

14 CRAB STICKS

5 OUNCES SNOW PEAS, TRIMMED

*6 USUYAKI OMELETS (SEE PAGE 14)
MADE WITH 4 EGGS AND 1/2 TEASPOON SALT*

*SUMESHI RICE (SEE PAGE 13) MADE WITH
1 1/2 CUPS RICE MIXED WITH 3 TABLESPOONS
RICE VINEGAR, 1 TABLESPOON SUGAR,
AND 1/2 TEASPOON SALT*

*6 OR 7 LEAVES FROM SMALL ROUND LETTUCE,
WASHED AND CUT IN HALF LENGTHWISE*

6 NORI SHEETS

*BENI-SHOGA (RED PICKLED GINGER),
TO GARNISH*

DIPPING SAUCE

1/4 CUP MAYONNAISE

1 TABLESPOON SHOYU

1 TEASPOON LEMON JUICE

◆ Preheat oven to 400F and cook bell pepper 30 minutes until skin is almost burned. Remove skin and cut flesh into 1/2 inch wide strips lengthwise.

◆ Insert a bamboo skewer lengthwise through body of each shrimp and boil in salted water 3 minutes. Cut in half along spine. Make a deep cut into crab sticks lengthwise to flatten.

◆ Boil snow peas in salted water 3 minutes. Thinly slice 3 snow peas lengthwise and reserve remainder for decoration.

◆ Put 1 usuyaki omelet on a makisu rolling mat and lay 2 shrimp slices end to end at front edge of omelet. Place bell pepper on shrimp, then lay 2 more shrimp slices end to end on top of pepper.

◆ Roll omelet following directions on page 31 and seal the end with a little crushed sumeshi rice to make it stick down. Make 3 of these rolls.

◆ Repeat the process replacing shrimp with crab sticks. Make 3 of these rolls. Set aside.

◆ Lay a nori sheet on the mat and spread a handful of sumeshi rice over it. Place a lettuce leaf in the center, place an omelet roll on top, and roll up (see page 31).

◆ Wrap roll in absorbent kitchen paper then press 5 chopsticks lengthwise at intervals around the roll. Secure with elastic bands at either end of the roll to shape it into a flower. Set aside 30 minutes.

◆ Untie rolls and cut each into 6 slices. Arrange to look like flowers on individual dishes with snow peas as stems and leaves.

◆ To make dipping sauce, mix mayonnaise, shoyu, and lemon juice together and transfer to a little dish.

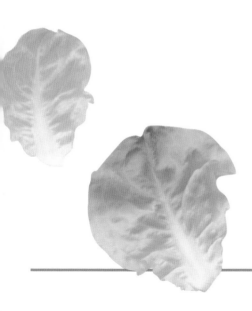

Ura Maki [Inside-out Roll]

MAKES 48

⅓ cup canned tuna in oil, drained and flaked

2 tablespoons mayonnaise

4 nori sheets, cut in half

Sumeshi rice (see page 13) made with 1 ⅓ cups rice mixed with 2 tablespoons rice vinegar, 1 tablespoon sugar, and ½ teaspoon salt

3 ounces fresh tuna fillet, cut into ½ inch square strips

¼ cup black sesame seeds, toasted

¾ cup tororo or oboro konbu (shaved compressed konbu, see page 11 and Note)

Gari and shoyu, to serve

◆ Mix tuna with mayonnaise and set aside.

◆ Wrap a makisu rolling mat with plastic wrap. Lay a piece of nori on the mat, shiny side down, and spread ⅓ cup sumeshi rice on top with wet fingers.

◆ Lift nori and turn it upside down on the mat so rice side is down. Make a thick horizontal line with 2 tablespoons of tuna mayonnaise 1 inch from front edge. Roll up. Repeat to make another 3 rolls.

◆ Make another 4 rolls, replacing tuna mayonnaise with fresh tuna strips.

◆ Evenly sprinkle 1 tablespoon of black sesame seeds over the mat. Place each tuna-mayonnaise roll on the mat and roll to coat evenly with sesame seeds. Set aside.

◆ Thinly spread tororo konbu to an 8 x 3 inch rectangle on the mat then roll to coat each tuna roll.

◆ Cut each roll into 6 and serve with gari and shoyu.

Note: Toasted white sesame seeds can be used in place of tororo konbu if the latter is unavailable.

Soba Zushi [Rolled Soba Noodles]

5 OUNCE SALMON TAIL FILLET, SKINNED

SALT

14 OUNCES DRY SOBA NOODLES,
PLAIN OR GREEN TEA FLAVORED

4 NORI SHEETS, CUT IN HALF

ATSUYAKI OMELET (SEE PAGE 27) MADE WITH
4 EGGS MIXED WITH 2 TABLESPOONS DASHI
STOCK (SEE PAGE 13), 2 TABLESPOONS SAKÉ,
2 TABLESPOONS SHOYU, AND 1 TABLESPOON
SUGAR, CUT INTO ¾ INCH SQUARE X 8 INCH
LONG STRIPS

GARI, TO GARNISH

DIPPING SAUCE

1 CUP DASHI STOCK (SEE PAGE 13)

¼ CUP SHOYU

¼ CUP MIRIN

1 TO 2 TABLESPOONS FRESHLY MIXED
WASABI PASTE

◆ To make dipping sauce, mix together dashi stock, shoyu, and mirin in a small pan, bring to a boil, then simmer 15 minutes. Let cool.

◆ Sprinkle salmon with salt and let stand 20 minutes. Cut into ¾ inch square strips 8 inches long. If fillet is not long enough, cut a few short strips to make up this length. Broil under high heat until color changes.

◆ Cook soba noodles following package directions. Drain into a strainer and wash under running water until cold. Drain.

◆ Place a makisu bamboo mat on the work surface, long side toward you. Cover it with a sheet of plastic wrap.

◆ With wet fingers, evenly spread a ½ inch thick layer of soba noodles crosswise on the mat. Lay a strip of salmon across the center and roll up, following directions on page 31. Set aside 15 minutes.

◆ Lay a nori sheet on the mat. Carefully remove plastic wrap from noodle roll and place roll on front edge of nori. Roll up. Repeat to make another 3 rolls with salmon filling.

◆ To make 4 rolls with omelet filling, repeat the above, but replace salmon with omelet.

◆ Slice each roll into 6 pieces just before serving. Add wasabi paste to dipping sauce to taste and serve with soba zushi.

Nori Maki Western

MAKES 72 PIECES

4 OUNCE PIECE COOKED HAM

3 ½ OUNCES GOUDA CHEESE

6 NORI SHEETS, CUT IN HALF

SUMESHI RICE (SEE PAGE 13) MADE WITH
2 CUPS RICE MIXED WITH 3 ½ TABLESPOONS
RICE VINEGAR, 1 ½ TABLESPOONS SUGAR,
AND 1 ½ TEASPOONS SALT

2 TEASPOONS FINE MUSTARD

4 SHISO LEAVES, CUT IN HALF LENGTHWISE

1 SMALL AVOCADO

LEMON JUICE

4 CRAB STICKS, SPLIT IN HALF LENGTHWISE

1 PACK MUSTARD CRESS, TO GARNISH

◆ Cut ham and gouda into ³/₄ inch square sticks.

u Put a makisu bamboo rolling mat on the work surface. Lay a nori sheet on it and spread about ⅓ cup sumeshi rice evenly over nori.

◆ Make a dent along the center with your finger and smear on a little mustard. Place a length of ham sticks crosswise on the rice and roll up following directions on page 31. Make 4 of these rolls.

◆ Repeat as above, replacing ham and mustard with gouda cheese wrapped in shiso leaves to make another 4 rolls.

◆ To make the final 4 rolls, peel and pit avocado, cut flesh lengthwise into ³/₄ inch thick strips, and sprinkle with lemon juice. Place avocado strips and crab sticks together and roll up as above.

◆ Cut each roll into 6 pieces. Wash mustard cress and cut ends. Scatter on each serving dish and arrange rolls on top. Dip each piece in mustard cress and eat with your fingers.

Smoked Salmon and Egg Sushi

MAKES 32 PIECES

4 QUANTITIES BASIC CHIRASHI MIX (SEE PAGES 47)

SUMESHI RICE (SEE PAGE 13) MADE WITH 1
⅓ CUPS RICE MIXED WITH 2 TABLESPOONS
RICE VINEGAR, 1 TABLESPOON SUGAR,
AND ½ TEASPOON SALT

1 POUND 2 OUNCES SMOKED SALMON,
CUT INTO 8 INCH LONG STRIPS

4 USUYAKI OMELETS (SEE PAGE 14) MADE WITH
3 EGGS BEATEN WITH A PINCH SALT

¼ NORI SHEET, CUT INTO 4 LONG STRIPS
LENGTHWISE

◆ Wrap a makisu with a large sheet of plastic wrap or a wet dish cloth.

◆ Mix chirashi mix into sumeshi rice and spread about ⅓ cup evenly onto the mat. Roll up following directions on page 31. Carefully unwrap and set aside. Make 8 rolls.

◆ Lay a quarter of the smoked salmon horizontally onto the mat to make a 7 x 8 inch rectangle. Put a rice roll on top of salmon and roll again. Make 4 rolls. Use crushed rice to fix the ends.

◆ Trim usuyaki omelets into the largest squares you can. Place a rice roll on top of one and roll again. Repeat to make another 3 rolls.

◆ Cut each roll into 4 pieces. Tie a piece of nori strip around each egg roll. Pile sushi on top of each other on each dish like a hay stack.

Ten Maki [Shrimp Tempura Roll]

MAKES 16 PIECES

*8 LARGE RAW SHRIMP, PEELED AND HEADS
REMOVED, TAILS INTACT*

1 EGG, LIGHTLY BEATEN

¾ CUP PLAIN FLOUR

PINCH SALT

VEGETABLE OIL, FOR DEEP-FRYING

4 NORI SHEETS, CUT IN HALF

*SUMESHI RICE (SEE PAGE 13) MADE WITH
1 ⅓ CUPS RICE MIXED WITH 2 TABLESPOONS
RICE VINEGAR, 1 TABLESPOON SUGAR,
AND ½ TEASPOON SALT*

*¼ CUP EACH WHITE AND BLACK SESAME SEEDS,
TOASTED*

SHOYU, TO SERVE

◆ Using a toothpick, remove black veins from backs of shrimp. Snip off very ends of shrimp tails with scissors and press to squeeze water out. (This prevents hot oil splashing when deep-frying.) Make a few slits across belly of shrimp.

◆ To make tempura batter, put egg, flour, and salt in a bowl and lightly mix using 3 or 4 chopsticks.

◆ Half fill a deep skillet with vegetable oil and heat to 340F. Hold tail of each shrimp and dip into batter then plunge into hot oil. Fry 3 or 4 minutes or until golden brown.

◆ Remove tempura from pan with a slotted spoon and drain on absorbent kitchen paper over a wire rack. Cool slightly.

◆ Wrap a makisu rolling mat with plastic wrap. Lay a nori sheet on top and spread with 7 tablespoons sumeshi rice. Turn it upside down and rotate 90 degrees so that shorter edge is toward you.

◆ Place shrimp tempura at the edge of nori nearest you, leaving tail outside. Roll up.

◆ Put white and black sesame seeds separately on dinner plates. Roll 4 rolls in white and 4 in black sesame seeds to coat.

◆ Cut rolls in half diagonally before serving. Dip into shoyu to eat.

Uzu Maki [Whirlpool Roll]

MAKES 24 PIECES

4 OR 5 DRIED SHIITAKE MUSHROOMS

2 TABLESPOONS SHOYU

2 ½ TABLESPOONS SUGAR

5 OUNCE COD FILLET

RED FOOD COLORING

4 NORI SHEETS

*SUMESHI RICE (SEE PAGE 13) MADE WITH
1 ½ CUPS RICE MIXED WITH 2 ½ TABLESPOONS
RICE VINEGAR, 1 TABLESPOON SUGAR, AND
½ TEASPOON SALT*

*ATSUYAKI OMELET (SEE PAGE 27) MADE WITH
2 EXTRA LARGE EGGS BEATEN WITH
2 TABLESPOONS DASHI STOCK (SEE PAGE 13),
2 TEASPOONS SAKÉ, ⅓ TEASPOON SALT, AND
2 ½ TABLESPOONS SUGAR, CUT INTO FINE STRIPS*

*⅓ CUCUMBER, CUT INTO THIN STRIPS
LENGTHWISE*

SHOYU, TO SERVE

◆ Soak dried shiitake mushrooms in warm water 30 minutes, then drain, reserving ⅓ cup of soaking water. Trim stems off and cut mushrooms into thin strips.

◆ Place mushrooms in pan with reserved soaking water, shoyu, and sugar and cook 10 minutes.

◆ Cook cod and make pink cod flakes following the directions given for cherry blossom sushi (see page 67).

◆ Place 1 nori sheet vertically on a makisu rolling mat. Spread a quarter of the rice over it, leaving ½ inch margin at the furthest side.

◆ Put 1 strip each of omelet, mushroom, pink cod flakes, and cucumber across center of rice and roll up from the side nearest you (see page 31). Repeat to make 3 more rolls.

◆ Leave rolls to settle at least 30 minutes, then cut each into 6 pieces. Arrange on a serving plate and serve with a little shoyu in individual dishes.

Tazuna Zushi [Rope Sushi]

1 SMALL CUCUMBER

SALT

8 MEDIUM RAW SHRIMP, HEADS REMOVED

SUMESHI RICE (SEE PAGE 13) MADE WITH
1 ¼ CUPS RICE MIXED WITH 2 TABLESPOONS
RICE VINEGAR, 1 TABLESPOON SUGAR,
AND ½ TEASPOON SALT

2 OUNCE SMOKED SALMON SLICE,
CUT INTO 2 X ½ INCH STRIPS

SHOYU, TO SERVE

◆ Cut cucumber very thinly lengthwise, sprinkle with salt, and let stand 15 minutes. Wash off salt and cut into 2 x ⅓ inch strips.

◆ Insert a bamboo skewer lengthwise into body of each shrimp to stop it curling. Boil in salted water 2 or 3 minutes. Remove skewer, peel off shell and tail, then cut in half along spine.

◆ Cover the makisu mat with a piece of plastic wrap or a wet dish cloth. Spread one quarter of the sumeshi rice over it and roll it as an 8 inch long cylinder (see page 31). Carefully remove plastic wrap or dish cloth from rice roll. Make 4 rolls and set aside.

◆ Wrap mat in a piece of plastic wrap, tucking ends underneath mat, and alternately lay salmon strips, 2 slices of cucumber, and shrimp side by side diagonally on the mat to make stripes. Repeat to cover mat.

◆ Put rice roll on top and roll mat again. Wrap plastic wrap firmly around roll and remove mat. Cut though plastic wrap into 4 pieces. Repeat above to make another 3 rolls.

◆ Unwrap plastic wrap and serve sushi with shoyu.

Chirashi

[Assorted Toppings on a Bed of Sushi Rice]

Chirashi means "scattered" in Japanese. This is a home-style sushi made in every household in Japan throughout the year. A dish for celebrating the change of season, for happy occasions, chirashi appears on the table in endless variations. Typically, sumeshi rice is mixed with preserved ingredients, then topped with a mixture of seasonal vegetables, egg, fish, or herbs. However, you can use anything as toppings and this is by far the easiest style of sushi to make at home.

BASIC CHIRASHI MIX

The basic chirashi mix given below is used in futo maki (see page 33) as well as in many chirashi and oshi-zushi recipes.

MAKES 4 SERVINGS

1 OUNCE DRIED KANPYO GOURD, RUBBED WITH SALT TO SOFTEN THE FIBERS, THEN WASHED

8 TO 10 DRIED SHIITAKE MUSHROOMS

3 TABLESPOONS SUGAR

1/3 CUP SHOYU

1 LARGE CARROT, PEELED AND CUT INTO MATCHSTICKS

1 TEASPOON SUGAR

PINCH SALT

SUMESHI RICE (SEE PAGE 13) MADE WITH 1 1/4 POUNDS RICE MIXED WITH 1/3 CUP RICE VINEGAR, 2 1/2 TABLESPOONS SUGAR AND 1 TEASPOON SALT

Soak kanpyo gourd strips and shiitake mushrooms together in warm water about 1 hour until soft.

Transfer to a large pan with the soaking water and bring to a boil. Reduce heat and skim any scum from the surface. Simmer 20 minutes. Add 1 tablespoon sugar 3 times at 5 minute intervals, shaking the pan each time to dissolve sugar. The kanpyo should look translucent after 15 minutes.

Next, add 2 tablespoons shoyu 3 times at 5 minute intervals. Continue to simmer until the liquid has almost evaporated. Set aside to cool slightly.

Take one third of the kanpyo and 3 or 4 shiitake mushrooms. Chop kanpyo into 1 inch strips; discard shiitake stalks, and thinly slice caps. The remaining kanpyo and shiitake can be kept in an airtight container in the refrigerator 2 to 3 weeks.

Simmer carrot 15 minutes in enough water to cover. Season with sugar and a pinch of salt. Combine with sliced shiitake and kanpyo, then mix into sumeshi.

Chirashi Bento [Boxed Chirashi with Two Dishes]

MAKES 4 SERVINGS

4 QUANTITIES BASIC CHIRASHI MIX (SEE PAGE 47)

SUMESHI RICE (SEE PAGE 13) MADE WITH
2 CUPS RICE MIXED WITH 3 TABLESPOONS RICE
VINEGAR, 1 ½ TABLESPOONS SUGAR, AND
1 TEASPOON SALT

2 USUYAKI OMELETS (SEE PAGE 14) MADE WITH
3 EGGS SEASONED WITH 1 TEASPOON SALT,
CUT INTO THIN SHREDS

¼ SHEET NORI, SHREDDED

2 CHIVES, CUT IN HALF

CHICKEN AND SWEET POTATO

1 LARGE SWEET POTATO, PEELED AND CUT INTO
2 ½ INCH CYLINDERS

1 TABLESPOON VEGETABLE OIL

1 LARGE CHICKEN FILLET, CUT INTO 4

2 ½ TABLESPOONS SHOYU

1 TABLESPOON EACH, SUGAR, MIRIN, SAKÉ, AND
TOASTED WHITE SESAME SEEDS

HAJIKAMI GINGER OR RED PICKLED GINGER,
TO GARNISH (OPTIONAL)

½ CUCUMBER, SLICED THINLY LENGTHWISE

FISH AND GREEN ONION IN MISO SAUCE

2 TABLESPOONS WHITE MISO PASTE

1 TABLESPOON SUGAR

1 TEASPOON EACH FINE MUSTARD AND VINEGAR

BUNCH GREEN ONIONS, CUT INTO 2 INCH STRIPS
AND BLANCHED IN SALTED WATER

2 ½ OUNCES VERY FRESH FLATFISH FILLET,
SUCH AS TURBOT, SKINNED AND SLICED THINLY
CROSSWISE, SPRINKLED WITH SALT

◆ Stir chirashi mix into sumeshi rice.

◆ To make simmered chicken and sweet potato, parboil sweet potato by putting it in a pan with enough cold water to cover, bring to a boil, then cook 10 minutes. Drain.

◆ Heat oil in a pan and sauté chicken until color changes. Discard excess oil then add shoyu, sugar, mirin, saké, and 2 cups of water. Bring to a boil and skim off any scum floating on the surface.

◆ Reduce heat to medium-low and add sweet potato. Simmer 20 minutes. Let cool in the pan, then drain and separate sweet potato from chicken.

◆ To make fish and green onion in miso sauce, mix miso paste with sugar, mustard, and vinegar in a small bowl and add green onion and fish. Let marinate 15 minutes.

◆ Fill 4 small (7 inch square) lunch boxes with chirashi rice, decorating with shredded omelet, nori, and chive.

◆ Put sesame seeds on a little flat plate. Dip cut ends of sweet potato in sesame seeds and stand upright in each lunch box. Arrange drained chicken behind and garnish with ginger and cucumber.

◆ Fill a small tea cup or saké glass with fish and green onion in miso sauce.

Note: Serve with a simple clear soup (see page 14), if desired.

Summer Chirashi Salad

MAKES 4 SERVINGS

1 1/2 x 1/2 INCH PIECE GINGER, PEELED

4 OR 5 SHISO LEAVES, CUT INTO FINE THREADS

3/4 CUP GARDEN PEAS

12 ROLLMOPS (MARINATED HERRING),
CUT INTO 1/4 INCH SLICES

1/2 SMALL CUCUMBER, THINLY SLICED AND
SPRINKLED WITH SALT

1/2 TABLESPOON WHITE SESAME SEEDS, TOASTED

GRATED ZEST 1/2 LEMON

SUMESHI RICE (SEE PAGE 13) MADE WITH
2 1/2 CUPS RICE MIXED WITH 4 1/2 TABLESPOONS
RICE VINEGAR, 2 TABLESPOONS SUGAR, AND
1 1/2 TEASPOONS SALT

3 OR 4 USUYAKI OMELETS (SEE PAGE 14) MADE
WITH 3 EGGS, SEASONED WITH 1/2 TEASPOON
SALT, CUT INTO THIN THREADS

GARNISH:

1/4 CUP RICE VINEGAR

2 TABLESPOONS SUGAR

1/3 TEASPOON SALT

3 MYOGA (SEE NOTE) OR 1 SMALL
RED ONION, TO GARNISH

◆ Thinly slice ginger, then slice again to make thin threads. Soak in cold water 5 minutes. Drain.

◆ Boil peas in lightly salted water 5 minutes, drain and cool.

◆ To make garnish, mix together rice vinegar, sugar, and salt in a small saucepan, add myoga or red onion, and simmer 5 or 6 minutes. Remove pan from heat and let marinate 30 minutes. Thinly slice myoga or onion lengthwise and set aside.

◆ Mix rollmops, cucumber, peas, sesame seeds, and lemon zest into sumeshi rice.

◆ Put rice into a serving bowl. Arrange omelet and shiso strips on top of rice like a nest. Garnish with myoga or onion and serve.

Note: Myoga is the flower bud of the myoga plant and has a distinctive minty flavor. It is available from some Japanese stores in spring and early summer.

Fukiyose [Autumn Wind-blown Garden]

MAKES 4 SERVINGS

SUMESHI RICE (SEE PAGE 13) MADE WITH
2 $\frac{1}{2}$ CUPS RICE MIXED WITH 4 $\frac{1}{2}$ TABLESPOONS
RICE VINEGAR, 1 TABLESPOON SUGAR, AND
1 $\frac{1}{2}$ TEASPOONS SALT

1 QUANTITY BASIC CHIRASHI MIX (SEE PAGE 47)

4 OUNCES SHIITAKE MUSHROOMS,
STALKS REMOVED

4 OUNCES SHIMEJI MUSHROOMS,
HARD PART OF STALKS REMOVED

4 OUNCES ENOKI MUSHROOMS,
HARD PART OF STALKS REMOVED

4 OUNCES CHESTNUT MUSHROOMS,
THINLY SLICED

$\frac{1}{4}$ CUP SAKÉ

1 TABLESPOON SHOYU

1 OR 2 CARROTS, PEELED AND SLICED INTO
$\frac{1}{4}$ INCH DISKS

1 PACK COOKED GINKGO NUTS OR
20 FRESH GINKGO NUTS IN SHELLS
(AVAILABLE FROM CHINESE AND JAPANESE
STORES IN AUTUMN AND WINTER)

1 BOTTLE SWEET CHESTNUTS OR
12 FRESH SWEET CHESTNUTS

EDIBLE CHRYSANTHEMUM OR
OTHER EDIBLE FLOWER PETALS

◆ Mix sumeshi rice and chirashi mix together well.

◆ Make shallow cuts on top of 6 shiitake mushrooms to form a white cross. Thinly slice remainder.

◆ Put all mushrooms in a pan and sprinkle with saké. Simmer, covered, over moderate heat 3 or 4 minutes until moisture comes out. Add shoyu and cook an additional 2 minutes. Let soak until needed.

◆ Boil carrots 3 minutes, then cut into leaf shapes using a Japanese vegetable cutter or a cookie cutter.

◆ If using fresh ginkgo nuts, put in a pan with a handful of salt and roast over low heat until shells start to crack. Remove shells and peel off translucent skin.

◆ If using fresh sweet chestnuts, score shell to break and steam 15 minutes. Peel off shell and brown skin using a knife.

Drain mushrooms and fold into sumeshi rice. Heap up rice on a plate and arrange whole shiitake mushrooms, ginkgo nuts, and chestnuts over rice. Decorate with carrot shapes and chrysanthemum petals.

Serve at room temperature with a clear soup (see page 14), if desired.

Hamachi Don [Yellowtail Tuna Sushi Bowl]

MAKES 4 SERVINGS

*1 POUND FRESH HAMACHI YELLOWTAIL
TUNA FILLET*

*1 1/2 x 1/2 INCH PIECE GINGER, PEELED AND CUT
INTO THIN NEEDLES*

2 SHISO LEAVES, FINELY CHOPPED

*SUMESHI RICE (SEE PAGE 13) MADE WITH
1 1/4 POUNDS RICE MIXED WITH 4 1/2
TABLESPOONS RICE VINEGAR, 2 TABLESPOONS
SUGAR, AND 1 1/2 TEASPOONS SALT*

1 TABLESPOON SHOYU

1/2 TABLESPOON WASABI PASTE

1 NORI SHEET

1/4 CUP WHITE SESAME SEEDS, TOASTED

GRATED ZEST 1 LIME

◆ Cut tuna into 1/4 inch slices across the grain. If fillet is thicker than 2 1/2 inches, cut in half crosswise again.

◆ Soak ginger in cold water 5 minutes then drain and mix with shiso into sumeshi rice. Divide between 4 bowls or soup dishes and flatten surface lightly.

◆ Mix shoyu and wasabi in a small bowl, adjusting amount of wasabi to taste. Cut nori sheets into 4 then tear into small flakes by hand. Put in a bowl and mix with shoyu and wasabi mix. Spread this on rice.

◆ Lay fish slices over rice and sprinkle with toasted sesame seeds and grated lime zest.

◆ Ask guests to drizzle about 2 teaspoons more shoyu on fish and mix well before eating.

Inaka Chirashi [Country Sushi]

3 OR 4 DRIED SHIITAKE MUSHROOMS

1 ½ TABLESPOONS SUGAR

3 ½ TABLESPOONS SHOYU

½ CARROT, PEELED AND SHREDDED

*1 TO 1 ½ CUPS DASHI STOCK
(SEE PAGE 14)*

3 TABLESPOONS SAKÉ

3 ½ OUNCES CRAB STICKS, SHREDDED

1 OUNCE FRENCH BEANS, TRIMMED

VEGETABLE OIL, FOR FRYING

*USUYAKI OMELET (SEE PAGE 14), MADE WITH
1 EGG BEATEN WITH A PINCH SALT,
CUT INTO THIN SHREDS*

*SUMESHI RICE (SEE PAGE 13) MADE WITH
3 CUPS RICE MIXED WITH ⅓ CUP RICE
VINEGAR, 2 TABLESPOONS SUGAR, AND
1 TEASPOON SALT*

◆ Soak shiitake mushrooms in warm water 30 minutes, then drain, reserving ⅓ cup of water. Discard stems and cut caps into thin strips.

◆ Put reserved soaking water in a pan with sugar, 1½ tablespoons shoyu and mushroom caps and cook 20 minutes or until almost all liquid is absorbed.

◆ Parboil carrot, then cook in dashi seasoned with 2 tablespoons of shoyu and 2 tablespoons of saké 3 or 4 minutes. Sprinkle remaining saké over crab sticks.

◆ Lightly cook beans and slice diagonally.

◆ Fold mushrooms, carrots, and crab sticks into sumeshi rice.

◆ Garnish with beans and shredded omelet to serve.

Sushi Parfait

MAKES 4 SERVINGS

*1 CUP DASHI STOCK
(SEE PAGE 14)*

2 TEASPOONS SALT

DASH SHOYU

¼ OUNCE ENVELOPE GELATIN POWDER

½ LIME

*1 RIPE PAPAYA, PEELED AND CUT INTO
SMALL CUBES*

*BUNCH CHIVES, A FEW RESERVED FOR
DECORATION, REMAINDER FINELY CHOPPED*

*SUMESHI RICE (SEE PAGE 13) MADE WITH
⅔ CUP RICE MIXED WITH 1 TABLESPOON RICE
VINEGAR, ½ TEASPOON SUGAR, AND
A PINCH OF SALT (SEE NOTE)*

⅔ CUP LUMPFISH CAVIAR OR HERRING ROE

*4 LARGE SCALLOPS, SHELLED, FRILLS AND
CORAL REMOVED, CUT IN HALF HORIZONTALLY*

*12 AMA-EBI SWEET SHRIMP, SHELLED AND
HEADS REMOVED*

◆ In a small pan, heat dashi stock and add salt and a dash of shoyu. Dissolve gelatin powder in water following package directions and add to stock. Transfer to a small bowl and let set 1 hour in the refrigerator, then crush finely with a fork.

◆ Cut 4 slices from lime and squeeze the remainder for juice. Sprinkle 1 teaspoon lime juice over crushed dashi jelly and remainder onto papaya cubes.

◆ Fill each of 4 champagne flutes or other tall glasses with about 1 tablespoon of jelly using a long-handled spoon. Sprinkle with 1 tablespoon chopped chives, then put 1½ tablespoons sumeshi on top.

◆ Add 2 tablespoons of caviar, 2 tablespoons of papaya, then 2 scallop slices. Repeat layers of jelly and chive, then add sweet shrimp. Top with more chives, then decorate with chive stalks and lime slices.

◆ Serve with long parfait spoons and mix well before eating.

Note: This quantity of sumeshi rice is more than needed for this recipe but it is difficult to cook a smaller quantity successfully.

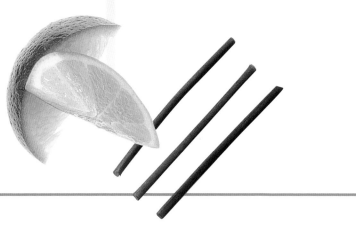

Checkerboard Chirashi

MAKES 4 TO 6 SERVINGS

8 OUNCES SMOKED SALMON SLICES

2 TEASPOONS SAKÉ

1 TABLESPOON SHOYU

SUMESHI RICE (SEE PAGE 13) MADE WITH
1 ¼ POUNDS RICE MIXED WITH ⅓ CUP RICE
VINEGAR, 1 TABLESPOON SUGAR, AND
2 TEASPOONS SALT

1 NORI SHEET, CUT INTO 2 INCH SQUARES

SHIO-KONBU (SALTED KONBU SEAWEED)
(OPTIONAL)

RED PICKLED GINGER AND SHISO LEAVES,
TO GARNISH

GARI AND SHOYU, TO SERVE

◆ Sprinkle smoked salmon with saké and shoyu then let marinate 30 minutes.

◆ Place half the sumeshi in a large container about 10 inches square and spread out to cover the bottom.

◆ Lay smoked salmon neatly on rice without leaving any gaps. Put remainder of sumeshi on top and press surface with a chopping board or similar flat surface.

◆ Lay nori squares to create a checkerboard pattern.

◆ Decorate with pieces of red pickled ginger and shio-konbu or remaining nori cut into chessmen shapes. Garnish with shiso leaves.

◆ To serve, slice with a sharp knife as if cutting a cake and lift slices with a spatula. Serve with gari and shoyu.

Jewel Box

*8 COOKED LARGE SHRIMP, PEELED AND HEADS
REMOVED BUT TAILS LEFT ON*

*12 ASPARAGUS SPEARS,
HARD PART OF STALKS REMOVED*

2 ½ OUNCES GARI, FINELY CHOPPED

*SUMESHI RICE (SEE PAGE 13) MADE WITH
1 ¼ POUNDS RICE MIXED WITH ⅓ CUP RICE
VINEGAR, 2 TEASPOONS SUGAR, AND
1 ½ TEASPOONS SALT*

*1 ATSUYAKI OMELET (SEE PAGE 27) MADE WITH
6 EGGS, CUT INTO ¾ INCH CUBES*

*12 OUNCES FRESH TUNA, CUT INTO
¾ INCH CUBES*

4 TO 5 OUNCES SALMON ROE

SHOYU MIXED WITH A LITTLE WASABI PASTE

◆ Cut each shrimp into 3 crosswise. Boil asparagus in salted water
3 minutes, then cut each spear into 4. Drain liquid from gari and dry on
absorbent kitchen paper.

◆ Divide sumeshi rice between 4 lunch boxes (6 inches square) and
flatten surface lightly with a wet spoon. Spread chopped gari on top.

◆ Mix omelet and tuna in a small bowl and distribute between lunch
boxes. Add shrimp and asparagus and top with salmon roe.

◆ Serve with shoyu mixed with wasabi paste. Mix all ingredients
together before eating.

Fruits Chirashi

1 LARGE PINEAPPLE

¼ CUP FRESH ORANGE JUICE

7 OUNCES COOKED AND PEELED SMALL SHRIMP

¼ CUP SLIVERED ALMONDS

1 KIWI FRUIT, PEELED AND CUT INTO SMALL PIECES

4 OUNCES STRAWBERRIES, THICKLY SLICED

4 OUNCES ORANGE-COLORED HARD CHEESE, SUCH AS RED GLOUCESTERSHIRE, CUT INTO ½ INCH CUBES

BUNCH CHIVES, FINELY CHOPPED

SUMESHI RICE (SEE PAGE 13) MADE WITH 1 CUP RICE MIXED WITH 1 TABLESPOON CIDER VINEGAR, 2 TABLESPOONS FRESH ORANGE JUICE, 2 TEASPOONS SUGAR, AND ½ TEASPOON SALT

FINELY PARED PEEL 1 LIME

GREEN SALAD AND CREAMY SALAD DRESSING, TO SERVE (OPTIONAL)

◆ Cut pineapple in half lengthwise. (Only one half is needed for this recipe.) Shave a little from uncut side of pineapple so that it sits stably on a tray.

◆ Run a knife around inside edge of pineapple then scoop out flesh. Remove hard core and slice flesh thickly into small pieces. Reserve ⅓ cup for this recipe and eat or reserve remainder.

◆ Pour orange juice over shrimp and let marinate 15 minutes, then drain.

◆ Toast slivered almonds in a dry skillet over low heat until golden brown.

◆ Fold pineapple, kiwi fruit, strawberries, shrimp, cheese, and chives into sumeshi rice. Heap up in pineapple shell. Sprinkle with toasted slivered almonds and garnish with pared lime peel.

◆ Serve with a simple green salad tossed in creamy salad dressing, if desired.

Mushi Zushi [Steamed Chirashi]

MAKES 4 SERVINGS

*3 USUYAKI OMELETS (SEE PAGE 14)
MADE WITH 2 EGGS AND A PINCH SALT*

4 LARGE RAW SHRIMP IN SHELLS

3 TABLESPOONS SAKÉ

1 PACK KABAYAKI EEL (PRE-COOKED)

3 OUNCES YOUNG LEAF SPINACH, WASHED

1 QUANTITY BASIC CHIRASHI MIX (SEE PAGE 47)

*SUMESHI RICE (SEE PAGE 13) MADE WITH
2 CUPS RICE MIXED WITH 3 1/2 TABLESPOONS
RICE VINEGAR, 1 TABLESPOON SUGAR,
AND 1 TEASPOON SALT*

4 CRAB STICKS, CUT IN HALF DIAGONALLY

*SMALL BUNCH MUSTARD CRESS,
STALKS CUT (OPTIONAL)*

◆ Roll 3 omelets together on a chopping board and chop finely.

◆ Put shrimp and saké in a pan with 3 tablespoons of water and boil over moderate heat with lid on 5 or 6 minutes. Leave in pan to cool. Peel but retain heads and tails.

◆ Cut kabayaki eel crosswise into 1 inch wide pieces.

◆ Blanch spinach in salted water 1 minute then rinse in cold water. Drain and squeeze out excess water and shape spinach into a small cylinder. Cut into 4 crosswise.

◆ Mix chirashi mix into sumeshi rice and divide between 4 bowls. Cover rice with a handful of omelet threads. Arrange spinach, crab sticks, eel, and a shrimp on top of each bowl.

◆ Cover bowls with aluminum foil. Heat a steamer and steam bowls 15 minutes over moderate heat. (If not all bowls fit in steamer, do this in several batches. Keep in a warm place).

◆ Garnish with mustard cress, if desired, and serve warm. Mix well before eating.

Hanami Chirashi [Spring Festival Chirashi]

MAKES 4 SERVINGS

3 TABLESPOONS SALT

4 SMALL FRESH MACKEREL FILLETS, BONED

$\frac{1}{4}$ CUP RICE VINEGAR

$\frac{1}{4}$ CUP CIDER VINEGAR

$1\frac{1}{2} \times \frac{1}{2}$ INCH PIECE GINGER, PEELED AND SLICED INTO THIN NEEDLES, SOAKED IN WATER 5 MINUTES, THEN DRAINED

1 APPLE, PEELED AND SHREDDED

SUMESHI RICE (SEE PAGE 13) MADE WITH $1\frac{1}{4}$ POUNDS RICE MIXED WITH $4\frac{1}{2}$ TABLESPOONS RICE VINEGAR, 2 TABLESPOONS SUGAR, AND $1\frac{1}{2}$ TEASPOONS SALT

12 LIVE CLAMS

3 TABLESPOONS SAKÉ

VEGETABLE OIL

3 EGGS, LIGHTLY BEATEN AND SEASONED WITH $\frac{1}{2}$ TEASPOON SALT

$\frac{1}{2}$ BUNCH CHIVES, FINELY CHOPPED

GARNISH

2 OUNCES DAIKON RADISH, PEELED AND THINLY SLICED

$\frac{3}{4}$ OUNCE GARI, PEELED AND THINLY SLICED

1 TABLESPOON RICE VINEGAR

1 TABLESPOON SUGAR

PINCH SALT

RED FOOD COLORING

◆ Spread a thick layer of salt on mackerel fillets and leave 3 hours. Wash off salt with water, then marinate mackerel in rice vinegar and cider vinegar 30 minutes.

◆ Meanwhile, make garnish. Shape radish and gari into cherry blossom petals using a Japanese vegetable cutter or small cookie cutter. Place in a small dish with 1 tablespoon each of rice vinegar and sugar and a pinch of salt and marinate an hour. Add red food coloring if desired.

◆ Remove fish from marinade, dry on absorbent kitchen paper and slice into $\frac{1}{4}$ inch thick strips crosswise.

◆ Mix ginger and apple into sumeshi rice and set aside.

◆ Put clams and saké in a pan and heat until shells open. Cool slightly and remove clam meat from shells. Reserve a few shells for decoration. Discard any unopened shells.

◆ Heat a little vegetable oil, add beaten eggs and cook, stirring, until finely scrambled.

◆ Mix mackerel and clams with sumeshi rice. Pile up mixture in a large serving bowl or on a plate and sprinkle with scrambled egg and chopped chives. Garnish with ginger and radish petals and serve.

Tekone Zushi [Marinated Seafood Chirashi]

7 OUNCES FRESH RED BREAM OR SNAPPER FILLET, BONED AND SKINNED

5 OUNCES COOKED OCTOPUS TENTACLES

3 ½ TABLESPOONS SHOYU

ABOUT 2 TABLESPOONS WASABI PASTE (ADJUST ACCORDING TO TASTE)

4 NORI SHEETS

SUMESHI RICE (SEE PAGE 13) MADE WITH 1 ¼ POUNDS RICE MIXED WITH ⅓ CUP RICE VINEGAR, 2 TEASPOONS SUGAR, AND 2 TEASPOONS SALT

3 TABLESPOONS WHITE SESAME SEEDS, TOASTED

BUNCH CHIVES, CUT INTO 2 INCH LENGTHS

◆ Cut bream fillet in half lengthwise then slice crosswise into 1 inch thick pieces. Slice octopus diagonally into ¼ inch thick pieces.

◆ Mix shoyu and wasabi and, using your hands, rub 2 tablespoons into bream and octopus. Set aside remainder in a small pot or milk jug.

◆ Tear each nori sheet into 4 pieces with your hands. (If it doesn't tear easily hold 2 sheets together and wave over a moderate flame a few seconds to dry it out. Alternatively, heat each sheet about 10 to 20 seconds in a microwave until crisp). Put nori into a small plastic bag and rub the bag to make rough flakes.

◆ Mix sumeshi rice with sesame seeds and heap up in a large bowl. Sprinkle over nori flakes, then scatter marinated fish on top. Drizzle with reserved shoyu and wasabi.

◆ Garnish with little bunches of chive and serve immediately, mixing ingredients well before eating.

Beef on Sumeshi Rice

MAKES 4 SERVINGS

1 POUND PIECE BEEF SIRLOIN

¼ CUP SHOYU

¼ CUP MIRIN

2 TABLESPOONS SAKÉ

1 TEASPOON SUGAR

2 SMALL ONIONS, THINLY SLICED ALONG FIBER

1 ½ INCH SQUARE PIECE GINGER, PEELED AND VERY THINLY SLICED INTO THREADS

5 OUNCES SNOW PEAS

SUMESHI RICE (SEE PAGE 13) MADE WITH 1 ¼ POUNDS RICE MIXED WITH 4 ½ TABLESPOONS RICE VINEGAR, 1 TABLESPOON SUGAR, AND 1 ½ TEASPOONS SALT

¼ CUP RED PICKLED GINGER

⅓ CUP WHITE SESAME SEEDS

◆ Put beef in freezer at least 2 hours, preferably overnight.

◆ Thaw frozen meat about 1 hour until outside is softened. Cut semi-thawed beef with a sharp knife into ¼ inch thick slices. Lay slices on a tray without overlapping and leave at room temperature until completely thawed.

◆ In a pan mix together shoyu, mirin, saké, and sugar with 2 tablespoons water. Bring to a boil and add onion. Cook 5 minutes or until onion is translucent. Add beef and remove pan from heat after 2 minutes. Stir and leave in pan.

◆ Soak ginger in water 15 minutes, then drain. Boil snow peas in salted water 3 minutes, then drain.

◆ Mix ginger into sumeshi and divide between 4 bowls or soup dishes.

◆ Remove beef and onion from pan using a slotted spoon and arrange on rice. Reheat sauce and pour over meat.

◆ Garnish with snow peas, sesame seeds, and red pickled ginger and serve immediately, mixing well before eating.

Oshi-Zushi
[Compressed Sushi]

Oshi-zushi is sumeshi rice compressed with toppings in a wooden mold. A cut piece looks like a slice of terrine. Marinated fish or pickled vegetables are often used as a topping for oshi-zushi. This style of sushi was developed in the western part of Japan and is closer in style to the ancient form of sushi, in which fish and cooked rice were compressed in a box to preserve them.

Oshi-zushi is easy to make at home and can be made before the day of serving—it will last 2 to3 days at a cool room temperature and some toppings taste better after a couple of days. Just 3 to 4 pieces are enough for a main meal for one person as quite a large quantity of rice is used. Eat oshi-zushi as it is with the fingers or using a pair of chopsticks.

HOW TO MAKE OSHI-ZUSHI

1 Wash the mold thoroughly. While it is still wet, line the mold with plastic wrap, making sure the top edges of the mold are covered by the wrap. If you don't have a Japanese mold, use a plastic container, roasting pan or glass oven dish, again lined with plastic wrap.

Place a topping at the bottom of the mold. If using oily fish, such as mackerel, press the skin side onto the bottom of the mold so that it comes out from the mold skin side up. (In some recipes sumeshi rice is added to the mold before the toppings.)

2 Fill up the mold with sumeshi rice and spread evenly with your fingers.

3 Press down with the lid and put a weight such as a heavy book or a large stone on top. Let stand 20 minutes to a few hours, according to the recipe.

Saba Zushi [Mackerel Sushi]

1 POUND 2 OUNCES MACKEREL, FILLETED

SALT

RICE VINEGAR

SUMESHI RICE (SEE PAGE 13) MADE WITH 1 CUP RICE, 2½ TABLESPOONS RICE VINEGAR, ½ TABLESPOON SUGAR, AND ½ TEASPOON SALT

LEMON WEDGES, MUSTARD CRESS AND GARI, TO GARNISH

SHOYU, TO SERVE

◆ Start preparing this dish 1 to 2 days before you plan to serve it. Place mackerel fillets in a dish, cover in a thick layer of salt, and leave overnight in the refrigerator.

◆ Remove mackerel and rub off salt with absorbent kitchen paper. Carefully remove all bones with tweezers. Wash off any remaining salt with rice vinegar. Using your fingers, remove transparent skin from each fillet, leaving silver pattern on flesh intact.

◆ Line a wet wooden mold or rectangular container measuring about 10 x 3 x 2 inches with a large piece of plastic wrap.

◆ Place a fillet, skinned side down, into the container and fill in gaps with small pieces taken from other fillets so mold is completely lined.

◆ Press sumeshi rice down firmly on top of fish with fingers. Put wet wooden lid on, or fold in plastic wrap, and place a weight on top. Leave in a cool place (not the refrigerator) a few hours.

◆ Remove sushi in plastic wrap from container, unwrap, and cut into small pieces with a sharp knife.

◆ Garnish with lemon, cress, and gari slices if desired. Serve with shoyu in individual dishes.

Cherry Blossom Sushi

MAKES ABOUT 12 PIECES

PINCH SALT

DASH SAKÉ

3 TABLESPOONS COOKED PEELED SMALL SHRIMP

2 TEASPOONS SESAME SEEDS

SUMESHI RICE (SEE PAGE 13) MADE WITH
1 CUP RICE, 1 TABLESPOON MIRIN,
¼ CUP RICE VINEGAR, 1 ½ TABLESPOONS SUGAR,
AND ½ TEASPOON SALT

WATERCRESS SPRIGS, TO GARNISH

DENBU FLAKES

3 ½ OUNCES COD FILLET

½ TEASPOON SALT

2 TEASPOONS SAKÉ

2 TABLESPOONS SUGAR

RED FOOD COLORING

◆ Sprinkle a pinch of salt and a dash of saké over shrimp.

◆ Heat a small dry saucepan and toast sesame seeds, then put them in a mortar and crush 2 or 3 times with a pestle to bring out flavor.

◆ Fold shrimp and sesame seeds into sumeshi rice.

◆ To make denbu flakes, cook cod fillet in just enough boiling water to cover, then drain. Skin fillet and carefully remove all small bones. Pat dry with absorbent kitchen paper. Using a fork, crush fish to make fine flakes.

◆ Put fish, salt, saké, and sugar in a pan and cook over low heat 1 minute, stirring. Dilute a drop of red food coloring with a little water and add to pan, stirring vigorously to spread color evenly.

◆ Lay some pink denbu flakes on the bottom of small flower mold and press some rice on top. Turn out onto a plate. Repeat until all fish and rice are used.

◆ Arrange as "cherry blossoms" on serving plates with watercress for leaves.

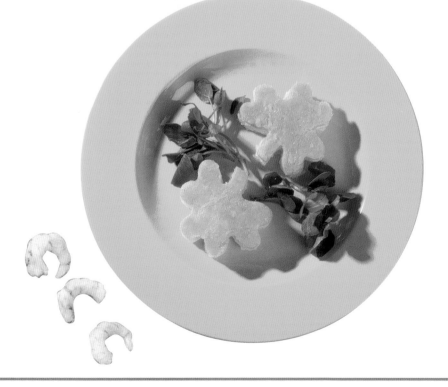

Bala Zushi [Harvest Festival Sushi]

MAKES 8 TO 12 PIECES

1 OUNCE DRIED SHIITAKE MUSHROOMS, SOAKED IN WARM WATER 3 HOURS

⅓ CUP SUGAR

¼ CUP SHOYU

4 USUYAKI OMELETS (SEE PAGE 14) MADE WITH 3 EGGS AND A PINCH OF SALT, CUT INTO ¼ X 2 INCH STRIPS

SUMESHI RICE (SEE PAGE 13) MADE WITH 1 ½ POUNDS RICE MIXED WITH ½ CUP RICE VINEGAR, ¼ CUP SUGAR, AND 2 TEASPOONS SALT

BUNCH WATERCRESS, WASHED AND STEMS REMOVED

RED PICKLED GINGER, TO SERVE

DENBU FLAKES

4 OUNCE COD FILLET

1 TABLESPOON SAKÉ

½ TABLESPOON SUGAR

PINCH SALT

½ TEASPOON RED FOOD COLORING, DILUTED IN 1 TEASPOON WATER

◆ Make denbu flakes following the directions on page 67.

◆ Place shiitake in a pan with enough water to just cover. Bring to a boil, then simmer 20 minutes.

◆ Add sugar and shoyu and cook until liquid has almost evaporated. Drain and remove stalks. Slice mushroom caps thinly.

◆ Sprinkle the bottom of large rectangular oshi-zushi mold or a square or rectangular container lined with plastic wrap with denbu flakes.

◆ Spread a third of the omelet strips, shiitake, then watercress over the top, then add half of the sumeshi rice and evenly spread with wet fingers.

◆ Repeat the process and finish with the third layer of denbu, egg, shiitake, and watercress.

◆ Put a heavy weight (such as a heavy book covered in plastic wrap) on the top of the container to compress. Leave at least 4 hours in a cool place. Do not refrigerate.

◆ Turn the container upside down on the chopping board. Slice the bala zushi into 8 to 12 squares and serve with red pickled ginger.

Soboro Oshi [Flaked Shrimp and Scrambled Egg Sushi]

MAKES 4 SLICES (2 SERVINGS)

3 TABLESPOONS SUGAR

3 TABLESPOONS SAKÉ

SALT

5 OUNCES PEELED AND COOKED SMALL
SHRIMP, FINELY CHOPPED

3 EGGS, LIGHTLY BEATEN

SUMESHI RICE (SEE PAGE 13) MADE WITH
1 1/3 CUPS RICE MIXED WITH 2 1/2 TABLESPOONS
RICE VINEGAR, 1 TABLESPOON SUGAR,
AND 1/2 TEASPOON SALT

2 TABLESPOONS AO-NORI
(GREEN NORI FLAKES)

2 SNOW PEAS, BLANCHED IN SALTED WATER
2 MINUTES, THEN CUT INTO THIN STRIPS

GARI, TO SERVE

◆ Put 1 tablespoon sugar, saké, and a pinch of salt into a pan and heat gently. When sugar has dissolved, add shrimp. Stir constantly with 4 or 5 chopsticks or a fork until the liquid has almost evaporated.

◆ Add remaining 2 tablespoons sugar and 1/2 teaspoon salt to beaten egg and pour into a pan. Heat gently and make very fine scrambled egg by stirring constantly using 4 or 5 chopsticks or a fork.

◆ Divide sumeshi rice between 2 bowls and mix ao-nori into one.

◆ Wet an 8 1/2 x 3 inch wooden mold and add ao-nori mixed rice. Press down with a lid. Add remaining rice and press with the lid again very firmly.

◆ Cover half the surface of the rice with a piece of aluminum foil 8 1/2 x 1 1/2 inches in size. Spread scrambled egg over the other half, then move foil to cover egg and spread remaining rice with shrimp flakes. Gently press the surface with the lid again.

◆ Remove sushi from mold and cut into 4 slices. Decorate with a strip of snow peas to separate 2 toppings. Serve with gari.

Sasa No Ha Zushi [Leaf-wrapped Oshi-Zushi]

3 OUNCES BREAM OR RED SNAPPER FILLET, BONED AND SKINNED

SALT

2 SHEETS KONBU SEAWEED, EACH 4 INCHES SQUARE

3 ½ OUNCE MACKEREL FILLET

RICE VINEGAR

SUMESHI RICE (SEE PAGE 13) MADE WITH ¾ CUP RICE MIXED WITH 1 ½ TABLESPOONS RICE VINEGAR, 2 TEASPOONS SUGAR, AND A PINCH OF SALT

16 BAMBOO LEAVES, ABOUT 8 X 3 INCHES IN SIZE, COVERED WITH A WET DISH CLOTH UNTIL REQUIRED

GARI, TO SERVE

◆ Start preparation 1 to 2 days before serving this dish. Sprinkle bream with a thick layer of salt and let stand half a day.

◆ Wipe konbu with a wet dish cloth. Sandwich bream between 2 sheets of konbu and refrigerate overnight.

◆ The following day, sprinkle mackerel with a thick layer of salt and let stand 3 hours.

◆ Wash off salt, then put mackerel in a shallow container. Pour on enough rice vinegar to completely cover. Let marinate 40 minutes. Drain, then cut crosswise into thin ¼ inch slices.

◆ Remove konbu from bream and cut fish crosswise into ¼ inch slices.

◆ Make a triangular shape with about 2 tablespoons of sumeshi rice. Press a slice of fish onto rice and wrap with a bamboo leaf. Repeat to use up all rice and fish.

◆ Place wrapped sushi triangles on their backs in a wooden mold, next to each other in a line, alternately pointing up and down so that the sides press together and the sushi form a solid block. Press from the top with a heavy weight and leave 2 hours or overnight in a cool room. Serve with gari.

Note: The leaves are used to infuse their fragrance into the sushi and are not edible.

Tartan Oshi

MAKES 8 SLICES

1 RED BELL PEPPER, FINELY CHOPPED

BUNCH CHIVES

5 ½ OUNCES FINNAN HADDOCK OR SMOKED AND DYED HADDOCK

PINCH SALT

PINCH SUGAR

4 OUNCES CANNED MUSSELS IN BRINE OR SHELLED COOKED MUSSELS

SUMESHI RICE (SEE PAGE 13) MADE WITH ¾ CUP RICE MIXED WITH 1 ½ TABLESPOONS RICE VINEGAR, 2 TEASPOONS SUGAR, AND A PINCH OF SALT

4 OUNCES SMOKED SALMON, CUT INTO LONG STRIPS 1 INCH WIDE

◆ Preheat oven to 400F. Roast bell pepper 30 minutes or until skin is burned. Peel off skin and cut into ¼ inch strips lengthwise. Keep 10 strips and finely chop remainder.

◆ Blanch chives in salted water 2 minutes. Drain and keep 5 or 6 stalks then finely chop remainder.

◆ Place smoked haddock in a large pan and just cover with water. Bring to a boil and cook 5 minutes. Drain, remove skin and any bones, then return to pan with a pinch each of salt and sugar.

◆ Over very low heat, stir haddock with 3 or 4 chopsticks or a fork until flesh becomes a fine fluff. This can take up to 30 minutes. Cool.

◆ Re-cook mussels 3 minutes in boiling salted water to shrink them. Drain.

◆ Divide sumeshi rice between 2 bowls. Mix chopped bell pepper and mussels into one and chopped chive into the other.

◆ Line an 8½ x 3 inch mold with a sheet of plastic wrap about 11 inches square. Fill with rice mixed with pepper and spread smoothly with wet fingers.

◆ Lay strips of salmon to cover the surface. Set aside 4 or 5 strips (enough to cover 10 inch length), and use up remainder.

◆ Fill up mold with chive-mixed rice. Put the lid on and press with a heavy weight 30 minutes to settle.

◆ Lift the lid and fill top of mold with ¼ cup haddock flakes. Wipe the lid very well. Press with the lid once again 5 minutes. If there is more space for the flakes after compressing, repeat the process until the mold is almost full.

◆ Gently lift the lid and decorate sushi in a tartan pattern with strips of smoked salmon, chives, and red bell pepper (see photograph opposite).

◆ Press toppings gently with dry lid. Carefully remove plastic-wrapped sushi from mold and cut into pieces with a sharp, wet thin-bladed knife.

Hako Zushi [Boxed Two-color Sushi]

MAKES 6 TO 8 PIECES

4 ½ OUNCES SALMON FILLET, SPRINKLED WITH SALT AND LEFT OVERNIGHT

3 OUNCES YOUNG LEAF SPINACH

6 ASPARAGUS SPEARS, BOILED 2 MINUTES AND TIPS REMOVED

SUMESHI RICE (SEE PAGE 13) MADE WITH 1 ⅓ CUPS RICE MIXED WITH 2 ½ TABLESPOONS RICE VINEGAR, 1 TABLESPOON SUGAR, AND ½ TEASPOON SALT

3 NORI SHEETS

GARI, TO SERVE

◆ Wash salmon and broil under high heat 8 minutes or until thoroughly cooked. Remove skin and break flesh into fine flakes.

◆ Blanch spinach leaves 1 minute then liquidize in a food processor. Drain into a strainer.

◆ Divide sumeshi between 2 bowls. Add salmon to one and spinach to the other.

◆ Cut 1 nori sheet in half. Put it on makisu rolling mat and spread with 4 to 5 tablespoons salmon rice. Roll up (see page 31).

◆ Put a whole-size nori sheet on the mat and spread about ½ cup of salmon rice on top. Lay the first roll at the front on top and roll again.

◆ Lay the other whole nori sheet into an 8½ x 3 inch wooden mold. Add about ⅓ cup of spinach rice and spread onto the bottom and sides of the mold.

◆ Place asparagus spears end to end along long sides. Insert salmon roll in the center and fill spaces with remaining spinach rice to completely cover the roll.

◆ Cover the surface with remaining ½ nori sheet and press firmly with lid.

◆ Remove hako zushi from mold and cut into 6 to 8 pieces. Serve with gari.

Shojin Oshi [Beets and Tofu Sushi]

1 pack (10 ounces) tofu

1 tablespoon sesame oil

1 cup dashi stock (see page 13)

2 tablespoons shoyu

1 tablespoon saké

1 tablespoon mirin

2 pickled beets, drained and cut into 1/4 inch cubes

Sumeshi rice (see page 13) made with 1 cup rice mixed with 2 tablespoons rice vinegar, 2 teaspoons sugar, and a pinch of salt

1/4 cup ao-nori (green nori flakes) or finely snipped chives

Cooked asparagus and bamboo shoots, to serve (optional)

◆ Wrap tofu with a dish cloth and put a weight such as a chopping board on the top an hour to dehydrate it. Cut in half crosswise.

◆ Heat sesame oil in a pan and fry tofu until surface has hardened. Add dashi stock, shoyu, saké, and mirin and simmer without a lid 15 minutes. Let soak an hour then drain through a strainer.

◆ Add beets to sumeshi rice and mix well.

◆ Wash an 8 1/2 x 3 inch mold and line with a piece of plastic wrap about 11 inches square.

◆ Put one third of the rice in the mold. Sprinkle the middle 2 inch width with ao-nori. Place 2 tofu pieces end to end on the band of ao-nori. Sprinkle tofu with ao-nori again and fill sides with pink rice.

◆ Fill up mold with rice. Replace the lid and put a weight on top. Let stand at least 20 minutes.

◆ Remove shojin oshi from the mold and cut into 6 slices. Serve with simmered bamboo shoots and asparagus, if desired.

Bo Zushi [Mackerel and Eel Baton]

MAKES 1 EEL AND 2 MACKEREL BATONS

*2 MACKEREL FILLETS,
EACH ABOUT 8 INCHES LONG, BONED*

SALT

RICE VINEGAR

*SUMESHI RICE (SEE PAGE 13) MADE WITH
1 ⅓ CUPS RICE MIXED WITH 2 TABLESPOONS
RICE VINEGAR, 1 TABLESPOON SUGAR AND
½ TEASPOON SALT*

*1 KABAYAKI EEL (PRE-COOKED),
AT ROOM TEMPERATURE*

HAJIKAMI PICKLED GINGER OR GARI, TO GARNISH

◆ Prepare mackerel (see page 66). Once skinned, put it on a chopping board, skin side down, and shave center of fillet lengthwise to make it flatter.

◆ Divide sumeshi rice into 3 equal portions and shape into rectangular blocks of the same length as the mackerel and kabayaki eel.

◆ Press rice into skinned side of mackerel and wrap tightly with plastic wrap. Repeat process with kabayaki eel, pressing rice into skin side.

◆ Leave "batons" to settle about 8 hours, then cut into 6 to 8 pieces still wrapped in plastic wrap. Remove from plastic wrap just before serving and garnish with hajikami pickled ginger or gari.

Sankaku-Zushi [Flat Fish and Omelet Triangles]

MAKES 6 PIECES EACH
OMELET AND SUSHI

*6 OUNCES FRESH FLAT FISH SUCH AS FLOUNDER,
SOLE, OR TURBOT FILLET, SKINNED AND BONED*

SALT AND RICE VINEGAR

*SUMESHI RICE (SEE PAGE 13) MADE WITH
1 CUP RICE MIXED WITH 2 TABLESPOONS RICE
VINEGAR, 1 TABLESPOON SUGAR AND
A PINCH OF SALT*

*1 ATSUYAKI OMELET (SEE PAGE 27)
MADE WITH 6 EGGS*

*3 LARGE COOKED SHRIMP, SHELLED, HEADS
REMOVED, CUT IN HALF LENGTHWISE*

6 SHISO LEAVES

GARI, TO SERVE

◆ Sprinkle fish with a thick layer of salt and leave 10 minutes. Wipe off salt using absorbent kitchen paper then cover fish with rice vinegar and let stand 5 minutes. Drain and wipe dry.

◆ Line an 8½ x 3 inch mold with a piece of plastic wrap about 11 inches square. Put fish into mold and trim to fit. Use trimmings to fill any gaps.

◆ Fill mold with sumeshi rice, put lid on and place a weight on top. Let stand 10 minutes.

◆ Cut omelet into 3 inch squares, then cut in half diagonally to make 6 triangles.

◆ Take sushi out of mold and cut into 3. Cut each slice in half diagonally.

◆ Arrange 3 pieces of each kind on individual plates. Decorate each omelet piece with a shiso leaf and each fish piece with a piece of shrimp. Serve with gari.

Other Sushi

The informal and enjoyable do-it-yourself style temaki zushi (see page 95) became a popular home party food in Japan about 20 years ago. Some say it was born in a sushi bar in California, others say it is a revival of the typical Tokyo Bay fisherman's lunch from the seventeenth century.

As sushi gets known and eaten world wide, there are a growing number of new sushi dishes appearing from all over the world. Ingredients from the West and other parts of the Orient can be used and dipping sauce is diversifying from standard shoyu to salad dressings. There is no limit to how high your imagination can fly in creating your own sushi menu. The only rule is always to use sumeshi.

HOW TO MAKE TEMAKI SUSHI

1 Pick up a quarter or half sheet of nori and place it diagonally across the palm of your hand.
Scoop some sumeshi rice with a small spatula or a tablespoon and spread it evenly on the nori.

2 Smear a small dab of wasabi in the center of the rice to taste.

Place up to 3 fillings of your choice, cut into thin strips, diagonally across the centre of the nori.

3 Wrap the nori and rice over the fillings into a cone shape. If using half a nori sheet, wrap it 2 or 3 times around the fillings.
To eat, dip the top of the cone into a dish of shoyu and bite. Nibble gari after eating each roll to clean your palette.

Canapé Sushi

BUNCH CHIVES

SUMESHI RICE (SEE PAGE 13) MADE WITH 1 CUP RICE MIXED WITH 2 TABLESPOONS RICE VINEGAR, 1 TABLESPOON SUGAR, AND 1/2 TEASPOON SALT

1/4 CUP WHITE SESAME SEEDS, TOASTED

2 OUNCES GARI, FINELY CHOPPED

RED AND GREEN LARGE THIN SALAD LEAVES

2 OR 3 USUYAKI OMELETS (SEE PAGE 14) MADE WITH 2 EGGS SEASONED WITH 1/2 TEASPOON SALT AND 1 TEASPOON SUGAR

CHICKEN & EGG CANAPÉ

2 TABLESPOONS SHOYU

1 TEASPOON MIRIN

2 TEASPOONS SAKÉ

2 OUNCES CHICKEN FILLET, SKINNED

2 EGGS, LIGHTLY BEATEN

1 TABLESPOON THICK CREAM

SESAME OIL

BUNCH MUSTARD CRESS, STEMS CUT

HERRING CANAPÉ

6 PIECES MARINATED HERRING, SLICED TO 1/2 INCH THICK

3 TABLESPOONS SOURED CREAM

LUMPFISH CAVIAR CANAPÉ

1/4 CUP EACH BLACK AND RED LUMPFISH CAVIAR

1 INCH LONG PIECE CUCUMBER, CUT IN HALF LENGTHWISE, THEN VERY THINLY SLICED

◆ Set aside about 20 chives and finely chop remainder. Add chopped chives to sumeshi rice with sesame seeds and gari and mix well. Blanch whole chives 10 seconds, then drain and cool.

◆ Using scissors, cut across top of salad leaves to make "belts" 2 inches wide and 7 inches long. If leaves are small, use 2 or 3 leaves to make up each length.

◆ Cut omelets into similar-size "belts". If desired, use pinking shears to make decorative cuts along the top edge.

◆ To make chicken and egg canapé topping, mix shoyu, mirin, and saké in a pan, then bring to a boil. Add chicken and cook over medium heat until color changes, then cover the pan and simmer 15 minutes. Add a little water if liquid gets too low.

◆ Remove chicken from pan, cool slightly, and chop into 1/4 inch cubes. Return to pan and let marinate until required.

◆ Mix eggs and cream well and season with a pinch of salt. Heat a little sesame oil in a pan and, using a whisk or 3 or 4 chopsticks, cook the mixture until soft and scramble finely. Cool, then mix in chicken and mustard cress.

◆ Make 18 nigiri-shaped rice blocks (see page 17) using about 2 tablespoons of sumeshi rice. Keep a bowl of water and vinegar mix nearby to wet your hands.

◆ Wrap 6 rice blocks with usuyaki omelet "belts" and stick ends down with crushed sumeshi rice. Tie with a blanched chive stalk.

◆ Wrap remaining rice blocks with salad leaf "belts". Use a toothpick to pin leaf to rice, then tie with a chive stalk and remove the toothpick.

◆ Top each omelet-wrapped sushi with 2 teaspoons each of red and black lumpfish caviar. Garnish with cucumber slices.

◆ Top each red leaf-wrapped sushi with 1 1/2 teaspoons soured cream and place a herring slice on top. Top each green leaf-wrapped sushi with chicken and egg mixture.

Sushi Candy

MAKES 12 CANDIES

¾ CUP GARDEN PEAS

SUMESHI RICE (SEE PAGE 13) MADE WITH 1 ⅓ CUPS RICE MIXED WITH 2 TABLESPOONS RICE VINEGAR, 1 ½ TABLESPOONS SUGAR, AND ½ TEASPOON SALT

12 RAW TIGER SHRIMP, PEELED AND HEADS REMOVED

2 TABLESPOONS RICE VINEGAR MIXED WITH 1 TABLESPOON WATER AND 1 TEASPOON SALT

4 ½ OUNCES SMOKED SALMON SLICES, CUT LENGTHWISE INTO 1 INCH WIDE STRIPS

½ NORI SHEET, CUT INTO 12 LONG STRIPS

FOR PRESENTATION

12 PIECES CELLOPHANE WRAP, EACH 9 INCHES SQUARE

RIBBON

◆ Cook peas in boiling salted water 5 minutes. Divide sumeshi between 3 bowls. Add cooked peas to one bowl.

◆ Cook shrimp in boiling water 2 minutes. Marinate in vinegar and salt mixture 20 minutes. Drain.

◆ Cut 12 pieces of plastic wrap 8 inches square. Line a Japanese tea cup or small coffee cup with a square of plastic wrap, then line with smoked salmon, leaving no gaps.

◆ Fill cup with about 2 tablespoons sumeshi rice and press firmly into cup with your fingers. Push one shrimp into the cup. Cover it with another 2 tablespoons of rice.

◆ Twist plastic wrap over cup and lift out contents. Hold plastic wrap and shape into a round ball.

◆ Repeat process to make 3 more salmon balls, 4 pea-mixture balls and 4 with plain sumeshi rice, each containing a shrimp.

◆ Unwrap plastic wrap from all 12 balls and stick 3 strips of nori to each of the 4 plain sumeshi rice balls. Transfer each ball to a square of cellophane wrap. Roll and twist to look like candy, then tie ends with ribbon.

Fukusa [Sushi Packages]

1 ½ INCH PIECE RENKON (LOTUS ROOT, BUY PEELED AND PARBOILED PACK), SLICED ABOUT ⅛ INCH THICK

SUMESHI RICE (SEE PAGE 13) MADE WITH 1 ⅓ CUPS RICE MIXED WITH 2 TABLESPOONS RICE VINEGAR, 1 TABLESPOON SUGAR, AND ½ TEASPOON SALT

1 TABLESPOON SHOYU

¾ INCH FRESH GINGER, PEELED AND GRATED

3 TABLESPOONS SAKÉ

1 TABLESPOON SUGAR

1 CUP (7 OUNCES) GROUND CHICKEN

12 LONG CHIVES

8 THIN USUYAKI OMELETS (SEE PAGE 14) MADE WITH 6 EGGS, LIGHTLY BEATEN WITH 1 TEASPOON SALT

4 SHISO LEAVES AND GARI, TO GARNISH

SHOYU, TO SERVE

RENKON SEASONING

RED FOOD COLORING

3 TABLESPOONS RICE VINEGAR

1 ½ TEASPOONS SUGAR

PINCH OF SALT

◆ To make renkon seasoning, mix rice vinegar, sugar, and salt in a pan. Add renkon slices and pour over enough water to just cover. Bring to a boil, then simmer a few minutes until renkon is translucent.

◆ Drain. Set aside 12 slices for decoration. If desired, dye 4 slices with red food coloring and cut in half. Chop remainder and mix into sumeshi.

◆ Put shoyu, ginger, saké, and sugar in a small pan with 1 tablespoon of water and bring to a boil. Add chicken and stir with a fork until liquid has almost evaporated. Cool slightly.

◆ Blanch 8 chives for 10 seconds in boiling water and finely chop remainder. Mix cooled chicken and chopped chives into sumeshi, then mold by hand into 8 rectangular shapes.

◆ Place a rice rectangle onto center of an omelet and wrap like a parcel. Tie a chive around center.

◆ Slip 2 colored renkon slices underneath. Garnish with a small pile of gari on a shiso leaf and serve with a little dish of shoyu.

Gunkan Maki [Nori-rolled Open-style Sushi]

MAKES 24 PIECES

3 GREEN ONIONS

1 TABLESPOON WHITE SESAME SEEDS, TOASTED

2 OUNCES FRESH TUNA (SEE NOTE),
CUT INTO ¼ INCH CUBES

1 TEASPOON LEMON JUICE

1 DRESSED CRAB, FRESH OR CANNED

SUMESHI RICE (SEE PAGE 13) MADE WITH 1 CUP
RICE MIXED WITH 2 TABLESPOONS RICE VINEGAR,
2 TEASPOONS SUGAR, AND A PINCH OF SALT

4 NORI SHEETS, CUT INTO 6 RIBBONS
1 ¼ INCH WIDE

1 TABLESPOON WASABI PASTE

4 FRESH QUAIL EGG YOLKS

GARI AND SHOYU, TO SERVE

◆ Reserve white part of 1 green onion and finely chop remainder. Cut white part 1½ inches long then slice thinly lengthwise.

◆ Add 3 tablespoons chopped green onion and sesame seeds to tuna and mix well. Sprinkle lemon juice onto crab and mix well.

◆ Make 24 hand-molded rice blocks following nigiri directions on page 17. Wrap a nori ribbon around each rice block and stick down the end with a bit of crushed sumeshi rice. There should be about ½ inch space between rice block and top of ribbon in which to put toppings.

◆ Smear a dab of wasabi on rice. Fill 8 of these "cases" with 1 to 2 tablespoons tuna and 8 with crab mix. Fill remaining 8 with strips of green onion, topped with a quail egg yolk. Sprinkle top of all 24 cases with chopped green onion.

◆ Serve with gari. Pick up with fingers, dip into shoyu and eat.

Note: You could use tuna trimmings from nigiri or maki-mono for this recipe.

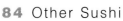

Chakin Sushi [Sushi in Pancake Wraps]

MAKES 12-16

1 OR 2 DRIED SHIITAKE MUSHROOMS

3 ½ OUNCES DRIED SHRIMP

3 TABLESPOONS SAKÉ OR WHITE WINE

2 TABLESPOONS SHOYU

2 TABLESPOONS SUGAR

2 TEASPOONS SESAME SEEDS

1 NORI SHEET, CRUMBLED

*SUMESHI RICE (SEE PAGE 13) MADE WITH 1 CUP
RICE MIXED WITH 1 TABLESPOON MIRIN,
¼ CUP RICE VINEGAR, 1 ½ TABLESPOONS SUGAR,
AND ½ TEASPOON SALT*

*12 TO 16 USUYAKI OMELETS (SEE PAGE 14)
MADE WITH 8 BEATEN EGGS, 2 ½ TABLESPOONS
SUGAR, AND 2 TABLESPOONS CORNSTARCH
MIXED WITH 2 TABLESPOONS WATER*

12 TO 16 SPRIGS WATERCRESS

◆ Soak mushrooms in warm water and shrimp in saké or wine 30 minutes. Drain mushrooms, reserving 5 tablespoons soaking liquid.

◆ Put reserved soaking liquid in a pan with shoyu and sugar, add mushrooms, and cook 10 minutes. Let cool, then chop finely.

◆ Meanwhile, drain shrimp and chop roughly if large.

◆ In a dry saucepan, toast sesame seeds and crush roughly.

◆ Mix crumbled nori, shrimp, mushrooms, and sesame seeds into sumeshi rice.

◆ Wrap 2 to 3 tablespoons of rice in an omelet, then tie up like a money bag with watercress sprigs.

Sushi Bento [Sushi Lunch Box]

MAKES 4 SERVINGS

*1 ATSUYAKI OMELET (SEE PAGE 27) MADE WITH
4 EGGS BEATEN WITH 2 TEASPOONS MIRIN,
2 TEASPOONS SUGAR, AND 1 TEASPOON SALT*

2 ROLLS TAZUNA ZUSHI (SEE PAGE 45)

*4 EACH SHRIMP AND SQUID EDOMAE NIGIRI
(SEE PAGE 29)*

NIMONO

1 CARROT, CUT LENGTHWISE INTO MATCHSTICKS

2 TABLESPOONS EACH SHOYU AND MIRIN

7 TABLESPOONS DASHI STOCK (SEE PAGE 13)

*1 1/2 INCH PIECE RENKON (LOTUS ROOT), SLICED
INTO 1/3 INCH DISKS, THEN CUT IN HALF*

KOBACHI

*2 INCH PIECE DAIKON RADISH, PEELED AND CUT
INTO 1/3 INCH CUBES, SPRINKLED WITH SALT AND
A SQUEEZE LEMON JUICE*

1/4 CUP SALMON ROE

*4 AMA-EBI (SWEET RAW SHRIMP), SHELLED AND
HEADS REMOVED, CUT INTO 4 CROSSWISE*

BUNCH MUSTARD CRESS, TO GARNISH

ASSORTED SASHIMI

*1/4 OUNCE EACH CARROT AND DAIKON RADISH,
PEELED AND SLICED VERY THINLY LENGTHWISE*

8 SHISO LEAVES

*2 OUNCES EACH TUNA AND MARINATED
MACKEREL (SEE PAGE 66)*

8 AMA-EBI (SWEET RAW SHRIMP)

2 LEMON SLICES, HALVED

◆ To make nimono, par-boil carrot slices 8-10 minutes. If using fresh renkon, peel and parboil for 15 minutes. Drain, then soak in one part water mixed with 8 parts rice vinegar for at least 20 minutes.

◆ Mix shoyu, mirin, and dashi stock in a medium pan and bring to a boil. Add parboiled carrots and renkon, cover pan, and simmer an additional 20 minutes. Drain.

◆ To make kobachi, mix together daikon cubes, salmon roe, and ama-ebi and divide mixture between 4 small tea cups. Garnish with mustard cress.

◆ To make assorted sashimi, pile daikon and carrot onto a small flat plate. Cut tuna and marinated mackerel into 1/2 inch thick rectangular slices. Arrange fish and shrimp on 2 shiso leaves and a half slice of lemon.

◆ Cut each tazuna zushi roll into 4 pieces. Cut omelet into 4 crosswise, then in half diagonally.

◆ To serve, arrange the various dishes as follows in a Japanese lunch box or similar-size box approximately 11 inches square. Place assorted sashimi in the top righthand corner, with tazuna zushi, garnished with gari, below. Place kobachi next to tazuna zushi. Stand 2 pieces of omelet in the top lefthand corner and lean nimono on them. Place 2 pieces of edomae nigiri below.

◆ If desired, serve with a simple clear soup (see page 14).

Note: Bento is the classic Japanese lunch box. It always contains an assortment of foods including a rice dish, fish or meat, vegetables, and pickles. Unusually for bento, this example is almost all sushi. Feel free to substitute other recipes in this book for the dishes included here.

Crystal Ball

4 LARGE OR 8 SMALL TURNIPS, PEELED

4 INCH PIECE KONBU SEAWEED

*SUMESHI RICE (SEE PAGE 13) MADE WITH
¾ CUP RICE MIXED WITH 2 TEASPOONS EACH
LEMON JUICE, ORANGE JUICE, AND SUGAR
AND A PINCH OF SALT*

*3 OUNCES CRAB MEAT, FLAKED,
DRAINED IF CANNED*

ZEST 1 LEMON

SAUCE

*7 TABLESPOONS WATER RESERVED
FROM BOILING TURNIP*

1 TABLESPOON SHOYU

1 ½ TABLESPOONS MIRIN

*1 TEASPOON CORNSTARCH MIXED WITH
1 TEASPOON WATER*

GARNISH

*4 ½ OUNCES SPINACH, WASHED
AND LIGHTLY BOILED*

1 TEASPOON MUSTARD

1 TABLESPOON SHOYU

◆ Slice top ¾ inch from each turnip to use as a lid and shave a small piece from bottom of each so they sit upright.

◆ Place in a large deep pan with konbu and cover completely with water. Bring to a boil, then simmer about 20 minutes or until soft and translucent.

◆ To make garnish, boil spinach lightly about 5 minutes, then drain, cool, and place in a bowl. Mix together mustard and shoyu and pour over spinach. Toss to combine and set aside.

◆ Drain turnips carefully, reserving 7 tablespoons of water from pan. Cool turnips slightly and scoop out flesh with a spoon to make hollow cups.

◆ Mix sumeshi, crab meat, and lemon zest and fill turnip cases. Replace lids and put in a hot steamer about 5 minutes to warm rice.

◆ To make sauce, heat turnip water to simmering point, then add mirin and shoyu. Gently stir in cornstarch mixture until sauce thickens.

◆ Arrange "crystal balls" on individual plates and pour sauce around. Garnish with spinach and eat with a spoon.

Inari [Sushi in Fried Tofu Bags]

10 ABURA-AGE (FRIED THIN TOFU)

⅓ CUP SUGAR

2 TABLESPOONS SAKÉ

4½ TABLESPOONS SHOYU

2 TABLESPOONS WHITE SESAME SEEDS, TOASTED

FINELY GRATED ZEST ½ LEMON

*SUMESHI RICE (SEE PAGE 13) MADE WITH
3 CUPS RICE, 5½ TABLESPOONS RICE VINEGAR,
3 TABLESPOONS SUGAR, AND
1½ TEASPOONS SALT*

*1 SMALL USUYAKI OMELET (SEE PAGE 14) MADE
WITH 1 EGG BEATEN WITH 1 TEASPOON SUGAR
AND A PINCH OF SALT, CHOPPED INTO
FINE SHREDS*

*5 SNOW PEAS, BLANCHED AND THINLY CHOPPED
LENGTHWISE*

2 TEASPOONS VERY FINELY CHOPPED GARI

*GARI, RED PICKLED GINGER, AND
SHISO LEAVES, TO GARNISH*

◆ Cut each piece of tofu in half crosswise. Make a tofu bag by gently rubbing a piece of tofu, then inserting a blunt knife in center of cut end to separate skin into 2. Make sure both sides remain intact. Repeat to make 20 bags.

◆ Bring a pan half full of water to a boil and cook tofu bags 2 minutes. Drain.

◆ Return tofu to pan with 1¼ cups fresh water. Bring to boil, reduce heat, and simmer 30 minutes. While simmering, add sugar in 2 batches, then saké, then shoyu, in 2 batches at 3 to 5 minute intervals. Let cool completely. Drain and squeeze out excess liquid.

◆ Add sesame seeds and lemon zest to sumeshi rice. Use sumeshi to fill each of 10 bags to about two-thirds full. Fold over bag openings and place on a plate, folded side down.

◆ To make open-style bags, fill three-quarters full with sumeshi rice, leaving space for toppings. Fold top edge inside slightly and top rice with omelet, snow peas, and chopped gari, leaving tops open.

◆ Serve garnished with gari, red pickled ginger, and shiso leaves and eat with the fingers.

Hina Sushi [Doll's Kimono]

10 SNOW PEAS, BLANCHED IN SALTED WATER

2 QUANTITIES BASIC CHIRASHI MIX (SEE PAGE 47)

*SUMESHI RICE (SEE PAGE 13) MADE WITH
½ CUP RICE MIXED WITH 2 TEASPOONS VINEGAR,
1 TEASPOON SUGAR, AND A PINCH OF SALT*

*8 USUYAKI OMELETS (SEE PAGE 14)
MADE WITH 6 EGGS BEATEN WITH
1 TABLESPOON SUGAR, A PINCH OF SALT, AND
1 TEASPOON CORNSTARCH MIXED WITH
1 TEASPOON WATER*

*1 LARGE CARROT, PEELED AND SLICED VERY
THINLY LENGTHWISE, THEN BLANCHED*

*½ CUCUMBER, CUT IN HALF LENGTHWISE,
SLICED INTO THIN RIBBONS*

1 OR 2 CHIVES

*RADISH FLOWERS (SEE PAGE 15),
TO GARNISH*

◆ Peel open snow pea shells. Keep 8 of the longest halves and chop remainder finely. Stir chirashi mixture and chopped snow peas into sumeshi rice.

◆ Scoop a golf ball size piece of sumeshi rice into your wet hands and mold it into a triangular shape about ½ inch thick. Repeat to make 8.

◆ Fold an omelet in half, the round part toward you. Place a strip of cucumber horizontally across the top, overlapping top edge of omelet by about ⅛ inch. Place a strip of carrot on top of this, overlapping top edge of cucumber by about ⅛ inch.

◆ Put a sumeshi rice triangle on top, pointed edge overlapping cucumber and carrot slightly. Fold edges of omelet (and cucumber and carrot strips) across rice triangle to make a "gown". Make 4 of these female dolls.

◆ Repeat the above but using carrot strips then snow pea shells to make 4 male dolls.

◆ Arrange a female and a male doll side by side on an individual tray. Following the photograph opposite, decorate each female doll with a chive and red pickled ginger to make a "tiara" and each male doll with ginger and cucumber to make a "hat".

◆ Garnish each plate with 2 radish flowers and some leaves, if desired. Put remaining sumeshi rice in a cup and serve with red pickled ginger and shoyu.

Sushi Italiano [Endive and Radicchio Sushi]

MAKES 4 ENDIVE AND
4 RADICCHIO SUSHI

1 ½ x ½ INCH PIECE FRESH GINGER,
PEELED AND THICKLY SLICED

BUNCH BASIL

3 TABLESPOONS OLIVE OIL

4 ½ OUNCES CHERRY TOMATOES,
PEELED AND DICED

PINCH OF SALT

SUMESHI RICE (SEE PAGE 13) MADE WITH
¾ CUP RICE MIXED WITH 1 TABLESPOON
LEMON JUICE, 1 TEASPOON RICE VINEGAR,
2 TEASPOONS SUGAR, AND ½ TEASPOON SALT

4 SLICES PROSCIUTTO HAM

4 ENDIVE LEAVES

4 RADICCHIO LEAVES

4 CHIVES, CUT IN HALF

PINCH OF COARSE SEA SALT

⅛ SHEET NORI SEAWEED, CUT
INTO 4 STRIPS LENGTHWISE

4 TEASPOONS BLACK
LUMPFISH CAVIAR

3 TABLESPOONS
MAYONNAISE

◆ Soak ginger and a few torn basil leaves in olive oil 30 minutes. Add diced tomato to olive oil with a pinch of salt.

◆ Set aside 4 basil tips for decoration, then blanch remaining leaves in boiling water 10 seconds. Drain and chop very finely. Squeeze off excess water, then add to sumeshi and mix well.

◆ Divide sumeshi into 8 equal portions. With wet hands mold 4 into nigiri rice blocks (see page 17) and 4 into round balls.

◆ Wrap each nigiri-shaped rice block with a slice of prosciutto, place on an endive leaf, add 2 sprigs of chive, and bind with a strip of nori. Use a few grains of crushed sumeshi rice to stick ends down.

◆ Place a radicchio leaf on a plate and place a sumeshi rice ball on top. Squeeze mayonnaise on top of the rice ball and scatter over 1 teaspoon caviar. Repeat to make another 3 radicchio sushi.

◆ Arrange an endive sushi on each plate. Discard ginger and basil leaves from olive oil and serve oil in a small cup to accompany sushi. Garnish with a basil sprig.

Temari

4 OUNCES FRESH WHITE FISH SUCH AS FLOUNDER OR SOLE FILLET, BONED AND SKINNED

SALT

8 LARGE RAW SHRIMP, HEADS AND SHELLS REMOVED, TAILS RETAINED

SUMESHI RICE (SEE PAGE 13) MADE WITH 1 CUP RICE MIXED WITH 2 TABLESPOONS RICE VINEGAR, 2 TEASPOONS SUGAR, AND A PINCH OF SALT

4 OUNCES SMOKED SALMON SLICE, CUT INTO 1 ½ INCH WIDE STRIPS

¼ NORI SHEET, CUT INTO VERY THIN THREADS LENGTHWISE

½ CUCUMBER, CUT VERY THIN LENGTHWISE, USE ONLY SLICES WITH GREEN SKIN ATTACHED

GARI, TO GARNISH

◆ Sprinkle white fish with salt and let stand 45 minutes. Wipe off salt and thinly slice by inserting a carving knife diagonally across fillet (see page 15).

◆ Boil shrimp in salted water 4 minutes or until they curl up completely. Cool quickly in cold water, drain. Cut in half across the back.

◆ With wet hands, make 24 small rice balls using 1½ tablespoons of sumeshi for each ball.

◆ Cut 24 pieces of plastic wrap about 4½ inches square. Place a square of plastic wrap on your palm and put a shrimp in the center, cut side up. Press a rice ball on the shrimp, then draw edges of plastic wrap over rice and shrimp, twist together, and shape rice and shrimp into a ball.

◆ Repeat to make 8 shrimp balls, then follow same directions to make 8 white fish and 8 salmon balls.

◆ Just before serving, remove temari from plastic wrap and decorate with nori and cucumber threads. Serve with gari.

Temaki Zushi [Hand-rolled Sushi]

MAKES 48

*ABOUT 14 OUNCES ASSORTED FRESH FISH
FILLETS, SUCH AS TUNA, SALMON, BREAM,
SNAPPER, SQUID OR CUTTLEFISH,
SMOKED SALMON*

8 MEDIUM RAW SHRIMP IN SHELLS4

*ATSUYAKI OMELET (SEE PAGE 27)
MADE WITH 6 EGGS*

½ CUCUMBER

*1 MEDIUM RIPE AVOCADO,
PEELED AND PITTED*

1 TEASPOONS LEMON JUICE

*SALMON ROE, SEA URCHIN, OR
LUMPFISH CAVIAR*

8 SHISO LEAVES, HALVED LENGTHWISE

MUSTARD CRESS, STEMS CUT

CHIVES, CUT INTO 3 INCH STRIPS

⅓ CUP MAYONNAISE

2 TABLESPOONS WHITE SESAME SEEDS, TOASTED

*SUMESHI RICE (SEE PAGE 13) MADE WITH 1 ¼
POUNDS RICE MIXED WITH ⅓ CUP RICE VINEGAR,
2 TABLESPOONS SUGAR, AND
1 ½ TEASPOONS SALT*

SHOYU, FOR DIPPING

12 NORI SHEETS, QUARTERED

¼ CUP WASABI PASTE

GARI, TO SERVE

◆ Cut all fish into 2 to 3 inch long sticks about ½ inch square and arrange on a large serving tray.

◆ Insert bamboo skewers lengthwise into shrimp to prevent curling and boil in salted water 3 minutes. Remove skewers, heads and shells, then cut shrimp in half across the back. Lay next to fish.

◆ Cut omelet, cucumber, and avocado into strips the same size and shape as fish. Sprinkle avocado with lemon juice. Place omelet and vegetable strips next to fish.

◆ Arrange salmon roe, sea urchin, or lumpfish caviar, shiso leaves, mustard cress, chives, mayonnaise, and sesame seeds in individual small bowls. Place small spoons in bowls of caviar or salmon roe, mayonnaise, and sesame seeds.

◆ Put sumeshi in a large bowl and cover with a damp dish cloth until ready to serve. Provide a few rice paddles or tablespoons in a glass filled with water.

◆ Pour shoyu into individual small dishes for dipping and pile cut nori on a plate.

◆ Each guest holds a nori in their palm and spreads it with sumeshi, adds 1 to 4 fillings and a dab of wasabi, then rolls it like a flower bouquet (see page 79), dipping it into shoyu before eating. Nibble some gari in between rolls to clean the palette.

◆ Good combinations of the above fillings include tuna and shiso leaf, shrimp and avocado with mayonnaise, atsuyaki omelet and caviar, squid and salmon roe with mustard cress, cucumber and avocado with mayonnaise.

Note: Almost anything can be used as a filling, provided it's not too watery. Try to cut all fillings into 2 to 3 inch long sticks. Other possible fillings could include: rollmops, smoked oysters, anchovies, ham, cheese, cooked meat, tartar steak beef, cooked dried vegetables (see page 47), boiled asparagus, pickles, and natto (fermented soy beans seasoned with shoyu).

Index